WHEN THE LORD REMEMBERS HIS OWN

When the LORD remembers His Own

Zechariah's Prophecy

An Introduction and Concise Commentary

by
Malcolm C. Davis

JOHN RITCHIE LTD
CHRISTIAN PUBLICATIONS

40 Beansburn, Kilmarnock, Scotland

ISBN-13: 978 1 910513 05 7

www.ritchiechristianmedia.co.uk

Typeset by John Ritchie Ltd., Kilmarnock
Printed by Bell & Bain Ltd., Glasgow

DEDICATION

To my good friend and brother in the Lord, Malcolm Blanche
of Wetherby, minister of the Word and bibliophile,
whose father-in-law valued the Prophecy of Zechariah
as his favourite Bible book.

Acknowledgements

I wish to thank the following people who have contributed to the publication of this book: Mr Fraser Munro of Kennoway Assembly, Fife, for editing the whole manuscript, and making many helpful suggestions for its improvement; Mr Thomas Wilson of Springburn Assembly, Glasgow, for writing the Foreword; Mr and Mrs Graham Stanley of Harehills Assembly, Leeds, for proofreading the text, and making helpful suggestions for its improvement; my wife, Ruth, for enabling me to concentrate on completing the project; and Alan Cameron, and other staff at John Ritchie Ltd, for their work of composition and printing.

Leeds, July 2014.

Foreword

Zechariah is a remarkably common name in the Bible. There is a king of that name and more than one priest, but only one prophet named Zechariah has penned a major book included in the Old Testament. Zechariah himself is an interesting character, as Malcolm Davis shows in *When the LORD remembers His Own*. Called to the prophetic office as a young lad, he continued to serve his God until Nehemiah's day. Zechariah's prophetic ministry ended two and a half millennia ago, but his Prophecy remains relevant today; indeed, as the author shows, there are unfulfilled prophecies set out in the book that bears Zechariah's name. However, its relevance is not related only to unfulfilled prophecies; it is a prophecy full of Christ.

As is noted in his other works, "This commentary has been written from a conservative Pre-millennial, Pre-tribulational standpoint, which accepts inspired Scripture at face value and believes that it should be interpreted as literally as is reasonable". He deals firmly with the claims of higher critics that the undated chapters 9-14 were written long after Zechariah's day. His robust defence of the unity of Zechariah's prophecy is necessary and should be carefully considered by the reader.

Perhaps because Zechariah's prophecy is, as George L Robinson identified: "the most Messianic, the most truly apocalyptic and eschatological of all the writings of the Old Testament", many have studied carefully the Book of Zechariah. Malcolm Davis offers reasons for carefully considering Zechariah:

1. It leads to an appreciation of Christ;
2. It reveals truth more clearly than other passages of Scripture;
3. Its lessons are timeless;

4. It deals with important aspects of the Tribulation period and Christ's Second Coming.

As in parallel works from the author's pen dealing with major prophecies, Malcolm Davis deals with the structure of Zechariah's prophecy in clear terms that young and old will find helpful. The terms 'Visions', 'Messages' and 'Burdens' are considered carefully. Following the helpful pattern established in his earlier works, there is a concise commentary for each chapter of Zechariah, so each of eight visions received in one night is considered and its symbolism interpreted. The four messages that answer the questions being raised at the time of writing are expounded, as are the two burdens (or oracles) with their clear prophecies about Christ. Throughout *When the LORD remembers His Own,* due emphasis is placed on the centrality of Israel and its promises. The promises made to Abraham and his seed relating to the nation of Israel's future, will be fulfilled when the LORD remembers His Own.

Before the eye of the reader, Zechariah sets out the glories of Jehovah's Servant, the Branch, the Stone, the King riding on the foal of the ass, the One sold as if He were no more valuable than a slave, and Jehovah's Shepherd and Fellow. The author does comment on the one pierced in the house of his friends: "It is probably not a reference to the True Prophet-Messiah, Christ, despite the clear reference to Him in the next verse".

The author has published several papers in academic circles including *Hebrew Bible Manuscripts in the Cambridge Genizah Collections.* His Concise Commentaries on Joshua, Isaiah, Ezekiel, Daniel and Revelation have been well received by a wide readership. *When the LORD remembers His Own* will also prove helpful to many.

Tom Wilson

Contents

Foreword	7
Select Bibliography	10
Preface	11
Introduction to the Prophecy of Zechariah	13
Concise Commentary on Every Chapter	31
Chapter 1	31
Chapter 2	39
Chapter 3	43
Chapter 4	48
Chapter 5	52
Chapter 6	56
Chapter 7	62
Chapter 8	66
Chapter 9	70
Chapter 10	76
Chapter 11	80
Introduction to Chapters 12-14	86
Chapter 12	88
Chapter 13	92
Chapter 14	96
Conclusion	102

Select Bibliography

In writing this commentary I have found the following books especially helpful:-

Lindsey, F. Duane. *Zechariah* in *The Bible Knowledge Commentary: Old Testament*. Editors: John F. Walvoord and Roy B. Zuck. Victor Books, 1985.

Feinberg, Charles Lee. *The Minor Prophets*. Chicago: Moody Press, 1976.

Hocking, Cyril. *The Prophecy of Zechariah* in *The Minor Prophets: their relevance for today*. Edited by Ivan Steeds. Precious Seed Publications, 1992.

Jensen, Irving L. *Jensen's Survey of the Old Testament*. Chicago: Moody Press, 1978.

The King James Study Bible, King James Version. Nashville, Tennessee: Thomas Nelson, 1988.

MacArthur, John. *The MacArthur Bible Commentary*. Nashville, Tennessee: Thomas Nelson, 2005.

Stubbs, John J. *Zechariah* in *What the Bible Teaches, Nahum-Malachi. (Ritchie Old Testament Commentaries)* Kilmarnock: John Ritchie Ltd, 2007.

Tatford, Fredk A. *The Prophet of the Myrtle Grove: an exposition of the Prophecy of Zechariah*. Worthing: Henry E. Walter Ltd & Eastbourne: Prophetic Witness Movement International, 1971.

Unger, Merrill F. *Commentary on Zechariah*. Grand Rapids: Zondervan Publishing House, 1963.

Unger, Merrill F. *Unger's Commentary on the Old Testament*. Chattanooga, Tennessee: AMG Publishers, 2002.

Preface

The main motivation for writing this concise commentary on the Prophecy of Zechariah has come from a friend and brother in the Lord who is in fellowship with the assembly at Harehills, Leeds. His late father-in-law in the North-East of England was especially fond of Zechariah's Prophecy and introduced him to its study. My good friend has in recent years urged me to consider writing a readable commentary on the book for the edification of the Lord's people, particularly to help those among them who cannot digest very detailed and lengthy commentaries due to lack of time for reading, but who are interested to obtain studies of the prophetical and other Biblical books which emphasise their main features clearly, concisely, and with some application of their practical and devotional lessons to us as believers today. There does still seem to be an interest in such commentaries as this one sets out to be, since my previous studies on the books of Revelation, Daniel, Isaiah, Joshua, and Ezekiel have so far been quite well-received by the Christian reading public. The present work will have achieved its aim and purpose, if both older and younger believers find that it has helped them to grasp and apply the main truths contained in the Prophecy of Zechariah with relative ease, and to enjoy the study of one of the most Messianic, that is, Christ-centred, prophecies in Scripture. If we fail to see Christ in the prophecy, and His relationship with God's ancient earthly people Israel, we shall fail to profit from the study, because Scripture states that there are clear practical lessons to be learned from them by us today as God's parallel heavenly people, the New Testament Church; see 1 Corinthians 10. 11; Romans 15. 4. Many of these lessons are drawn from the prophecy in the commentary and applied to ourselves in the twenty-first century AD, for all Scripture prophecy is intended to have a deep moral and practical effect on its readers' daily lives. That is the main reason why it was given to us in the first place.

This commentary has been written from a conservative Pre-millennial, Pre-tribulational standpoint, which accepts inspired Scripture at face value and believes that it should be interpreted as literally as is reasonable. The Prophecy of Zechariah includes many apocalyptic passages, some of which contain symbolical language in the prophet's visions of the future. These have been interpreted to refer to literal people, objects, and events; not to vague abstract ideas. In some visions the symbols are interpreted within the prophecy itself, while those that are not can sometimes be understood from parallel passages in the remainder of Scripture. Where it is not possible to be dogmatic about the significance of some aspects of a vision or prophetic message, a cautious approach has been made to understanding its meaning, and the main possible interpretations are given, leaving the readers to form their own conclusions with the aid of the Holy Spirit who inspired Zechariah to write them down. The prophecy does contain at least a few somewhat obscure verses, but the majority of the book is quite clear to believing readers. The main problem in understanding the book is our slowness to believe and accept what God has revealed in the prophecy, since some clear passages may seem to our 'little faith' somewhat incredible and unlikely to be meant literally. Believing readers will, however, accept the word of Almighty God as absolutely true and certain to be fulfilled quite literally in its right time.

Introduction to the Prophecy of Zechariah

1. Its Authorship, Background, and Date

The prophecy of Zechariah begins with the words: 'In the eighth month, in the second year of Darius, came the word of the LORD unto Zechariah, the son of Berechiah, the son of Iddo the prophet, saying,...'; Zechariah 1. 1. From Nehemiah chapter 12 verses 4 and 16 we learn that Zechariah was a Levite born in Babylon during the Jews' time of exile there. Thus he was a priest as well as a prophet, as were Jeremiah and Ezekiel. Zechariah was one of the three post-exilic prophets, together with Haggai and Malachi. Here he is said to be the son of Berechiah, who was the son of Iddo, but the references to him in Ezra and Nehemiah all call him the son, or descendant, of Iddo, rather than Berechiah; see Ezra 5. 1; 6. 14; Nehemiah 12. 4 and 16. This may imply that his father Berechiah had died young, and that Zechariah became the successor of his grandfather Iddo. Zechariah's name is a common one in the Old Testament, being shared with nearly 30 other men. It means, 'the LORD remembers'.

Duane Lindsey points out that Zechariah was a contemporary of Haggai the prophet, Zerubbabel the governor, and Joshua the high priest, and he returned from Babylon to Jerusalem with nearly 50,000 other Jewish exiles in 536 BC. At the time when he returned, he was probably a young boy, and even at the start of his prophetic ministry he was still a relatively young man, whereas Haggai may have been considerably older.

We note from the first verse of his prophecy that he dates his messages from the LORD according to the years of the Persian king Darius I, who ruled his world empire between 521 and 486 BC. The kingdom of Judah had been conquered three times by the

Gentile king of Babylon, Nebuchadnezzar, in 605, 597, and 586 BC. The rule of the Davidic dynasty had been interrupted from that time, and the citizens of Judah had largely been carried into exile in Babylon for a period of 70 years as a measure of the LORD's divine discipline for all their many persistent sins against Him. Now God was reckoning His people's history according to the dates of the Gentile kings and the so-called 'Times of the Gentiles' had begun, during which Jerusalem and Israel were to be subject to Gentile rule. This will continue to be the case until the second coming of Christ to reign over the whole world.

The Persian king Cyrus the Great had conquered the Babylonians in 539 BC and immediately encouraged the exiles to return to Jerusalem and rebuild their temple, which Nebuchadnezzar had completely destroyed. Sadly, only a small proportion of the Jewish exiles wanted to return from captivity. Those who did return laid the foundation of the temple and started to offer sacrifices on a rebuilt altar, but were soon deterred by external opposition to the work and internal depression, so that the work of rebuilding lapsed for about 16 years. Then the LORD raised up the prophets Haggai and Zechariah to exhort and encourage the returned Jews to continue the work in spite of difficulties and opposition. Haggai's ministry began first, in the early part of Darius' second year, 520 BC, and he preached four sermons in quick succession, exhorting the people to recommence the work. Zechariah's ministry began in the eighth month of the same year, that is, October-November 520 BC. His earlier, dated, messages continued until 518 BC, then his two longer, undated, messages were probably given much later in his life. According to Jewish tradition, Zechariah became a member of the Great Synagogue, a council of 120 members originated by Nehemiah, and presided over by Ezra. This council later developed into the ruling body of elders of Israel, called the Sanhedrin. Although we do not know when Zechariah died, Jewish tradition again states that he was martyred between the temple and the altar, as was an earlier prophet named Zechariah, who was stoned to death, according to 2 Chronicles 24.21. Zechariah's ministry was more one of encouragement to the returned exiles to finish the work than that of Haggai, who severely rebuked them for their apathy. Zechariah was led to motivate his people to restart the building of the temple by revealing to them the LORD's plans for Israel's long-term future. The two prophets succeeded in encouraging the exiles to restart building, and the second Jewish temple was dedicated on 12th March 515 BC. Not all the LORD's prophets in Old Testament times had such a rewarding response to their ministry as did Haggai and Zechariah.

2. Its Unity

Because chapters 9-14 of Zechariah are undated and have a somewhat different literary style from that of the earlier chapters of the prophecy, some commentators have attributed them to a pre-exilic writer, such as Jeremiah. However, higher critics have usually argued for a much later date for those chapters, namely, a time much later than Zechariah's day, about the third century BC, because of the reference to Greece in chapter 9 verse 13. But conservative scholars, such as Merrill F. Unger, have successfully answered all the critics' arguments by pointing out that Zechariah uses similar rare expressions in all three major sections of his book, and that stylistic differences between the major sections of the prophecy can be satisfactorily accounted for by differences in subject matter, and probably a much later period in Zechariah's life for chapters 9-14. Also, the divine name 'the LORD of hosts', although it is found most frequently in chapters 1-6, occurs in all three major sections of the book, thus tending to confirm the unity of the prophecy's authorship. In both Ezekiel and Daniel, the two captivity prophecies, this divine name had been conspicuous by its absence, whereas it had occurred very frequently in the earlier pre-exilic prophecies of Isaiah and Jeremiah.

The reference to Greece is no problem to believers, who accept the reality of predictive prophecy. At most, it reflects a date in the latter part of Darius' reign, or in the reign of his successor, Xerxes (ca. 486-465 BC), the Ahasuerus of the Book of Esther, who both waged wars against the Greeks. In any case, a large part of the book comprises predictive prophecy extending from Zechariah's day right through to the first and second comings of Christ. Therefore, although there are definitely three rather different sections within the Prophecy of Zechariah, namely chapters 1-6, 7-8, and 9-14, there is good reason to believe that they were all written by the one prophet Zechariah in the later sixth century BC and during the earlier part of the fifth century BC.

3. Its Literary Styles

The majority of Zechariah's prophecy is written in prose, but there are several sections written in poetry, namely, first a long one in chapter 9 verse 1 through to chapter 11 verse 3, then two much shorter sections in chapter 11 verse 17 and chapter 13 verses 7-9. As Duane Lindsey explains, Zechariah's style is characterised by epitome and much figurative language. He summarised many of his predecessors' prophetic themes, but showed creative individuality in the expression of the revelation of the future which the Holy Spirit inspired him to communicate to his readers.

There are two main exhortatory sections in the book: first, chapter 1 verses 1-6, and secondly, chapters 7-8. The vast majority of the book, however, comprises purely predictive prophecies concerning Israel and Christ, much of it also apocalyptic in character. Zechariah is one of the most apocalyptic and Messianic prophecies in the Old Testament. Other such prophecies include Daniel, Ezekiel, and Isaiah. Furthermore, the eight visions concerning Israel's encouraging future given to Zechariah in chapters 1-6 include much symbolism in their reference to historical people, places, and objects. Therefore, we can say that the prophecy of Zechariah is one of literary merit, full of interest and significance for the people of God, and has been presented to us in a very varied and interesting manner.

4. Its Outline Analysis

Two slightly differing outlines are presented here to interested readers, in order to help them gain a bird's-eye view and overall grasp of the whole prophecy. The first one is slightly shorter than the second one. It is that given in *The New Unger's Bible Dictionary* (1988), based on the work of Merrill F. Unger, whereas the second one is the outline given by F. Duane Lindsey in *The Bible Knowledge Commentary: Old Testament* (1985), which was edited by John F. Walvoord and Roy B. Zuck. The outlines read as follows:-

Merrill F. Unger's Outline of Zechariah

I. Call to repentance (1: 1-6)

II. Foregleams of the future Messianic Kingdom (1: 7-8:23)

    A. A series of eight night visions (1: 7-6: 8)

        1. The Man among the myrtle trees (1: 7-17)

        2. The four horns and craftsmen (AV 'carpenters') (1: 18-21)

        3. The Man with the measuring line (2: 1-13)

        4. The cleansing of the high priest (3: 1-10)

        5. The lampstand (AV 'candlestick') and the two olive branches (4: 1-14)

        6. The flying scroll (AV 'roll') (5: 1-4)

        7. The woman and the ephah (5: 5-11)

        8. The four chariots (6: 1-8)

    B. The symbolical crowning of the high priest (6: 9-15)

    C. The answer to the question of the feasts (7: 1-8: 23)

        1. The question and divine reply (7: 1-14)

        2. Future restoration of Jerusalem (8: 1-5)

        3. Future return to Palestine (8: 6-8)

        4. Kingdom prosperity of land and people (8: 9-23)

III. Two prophetic burdens: Israel's great Messianic future (9: 1-14: 21)

    A. The first burden: The first advent and rejection of the Messiah-King (9: 1-11: 17)

        1. The advent (9: 1-10: 12)

        2. The rejection (11: 1-17)

    B. The second burden: The second advent and acceptance of the Messiah-King (12:1-14: 21)

        1. Future deliverance and national conversion of Israel (12: 1-13: 9)

        2. The Messiah-King's return in glory (14: 1-21)

F. Duane Lindsey's Outline

I. The Eight Symbolic Visions (Chaps. 1-6)

    A. The introduction to the visions (1: 1-6)

        1. Preface to the call to repentance (1: 1)

        2. Particulars of the call to repentance (1: 2-6)

    B. The communication of the visions (1: 7-6: 8)

        1. The vision of the red-horse Rider among the myrtles (1: 7-17)

        2. The vision of the four horns and the four craftsmen (AV 'carpenters') (1:18-21)

        3. The vision of the Surveyor with the measuring line (Chap. 2)

        4. The vision of the cleansing and crowning of Joshua (Chap. 3)

        5. The vision of the gold lampstand (AV 'candlestick') and the two olive trees (Chap. 4)

        6. The vision of the flying scroll (AV 'roll') (5: 1-4)

        7. The vision of the woman in the ephah (5: 5-11)

        8. The vision of the four chariots (6: 1-8)

    C. The symbolic act concluding the vision (6: 9-15)

        1. The symbolic crowning (6: 9-11)

        2. The prophetic message (6: 12-13)

        3. The visible memorial (6: 14)

        4. The universal significance (6: 15)

II. The Four Explanatory Messages (Chaps. 7-8)

    A. The messages required by the question about fasting (7: 1-3)

    B. The messages declared as the answer from the LORD (7: 4-8: 23)

        1. A message of rebuke (7: 4-7)

        2. A message of repentance (7: 8-14)

        3. A message of restoration (8: 1-17)

        4. A message of rejoicing (8: 18-23)

III.   Two Revelatory Oracles (Chaps. 9-14)

    A.   The anointed King rejected (Chaps. 9-11)

        1.   The intervening judgements on nations surrounding Israel (9: 1-8)

        2.   The blessings of the Messiah (9: 9-10: 12)

        3.   The rejection of the Good Shepherd and its consequences for Israel (Chap. 11)

    B.   The rejected King enthroned (Chaps. 12-14)

        1.   The redemption of Israel (Chaps. 12-13)

        2.   The return of the King (Chap. 14)

5. Its Message

It has been helpfully pointed out that the key to the message of Zechariah's Prophecy 'hangs by the door' of the book, that is, in the opening verse, in the meanings of the names found there in association with the prophet himself. The name Zechariah means 'the LORD remembers', while his father's name, Berechiah, means 'the LORD blesses', and his grandfather's name, Iddo, means 'at His appointed time'. These names neatly summarise the main message of Zechariah's Prophecy, which is that the LORD is now remembering His people Israel after their 70 years of captivity in Babylon, and is promising to bless them again at His appointed time, both in the nearer future and in the far-distant future. Whilst there is emphasis laid on the need for God's people to repent and change their ways following suffering His discipline in captivity, the major theme of the prophecy is God's sovereign restoration for Israel and their consequent enjoyment of peace and glory in their Promised Land again, after Christ has effected their conversion and cleansing, and delivered them from all their enemies, at His second coming in glory and power to reign over His Millennial Kingdom.

Zechariah's Prophecy includes certain keywords which emphasise this theme of restoration for the LORD's downtrodden people. The first of these is the word 'jealous', or 'jealousy', applied to the LORD's attitude towards His chastened people Israel. It has a double significance in this prophecy, and elsewhere in the Old Testament. God first described Himself as 'jealous' when He made

His conditional covenant of law with them at Sinai; see Exodus 20: 5; 34: 14. He cannot tolerate His people having any other so-called god besides Himself. Consequently, when Israel fell into serious and persistent idolatry before the Babylonian Exile, His jealousy for them expressed itself in their severe chastisement, as was predicted in Deuteronomy 29 verses 18-28, and also stated in Ezekiel 5 verse 13, where the word 'zeal' in the AV translates the same Hebrew word for jealousy, *qin'ah*. In Zechariah chapter 8 verse 2 the LORD affirms that 'I was jealous for Zion with great jealousy, and I was jealous for her with great fury', in this same sense. God will not tolerate a rival to His people's affections and loyalty, and will punish them severely for any sin of idolatry. But His jealousy also works the other way, in favour of His redeemed people and against their enemies. Zechariah strikes this keynote early and clearly in his prophecy in chapter 1 verse 14, when he quotes the LORD as saying, 'I am jealous for Jerusalem and for Zion with a great jealousy'. He cannot tolerate anyone mistreating His people Israel without good reason and His own sovereign permission. Furthermore, in chapter 2 verse 8 the LORD states concerning the Gentile nations who had been oppressing His people, 'he that toucheth you toucheth the apple of His eye'. Israel is still the LORD's own special earthly people, and in this prophecy He promises to fully restore them to favour and blessing in Christ's Millennial Kingdom.

The other main keyword of Zechariah's Prophecy is the name of the LORD which he most frequently uses to refer to Him, namely, 'the LORD of hosts'. This occurs 52 times throughout the prophecy, 20 times in chapters 1-6 and 32 times in chapters 7-14. It has already been pointed out that this divine name was not used at all by the two captivity prophets, Ezekiel and Daniel, because Israel was then under the LORD's discipline and not yet eligible for His deliverance or blessing. This name is first found in Scripture in 1 Samuel chapter 1 verse 3, and in verse 11 in Hannah's prayer for a son to relieve her affliction of barrenness and consequent persecution by her rival wife, Peninnah. This first reference is the key to understanding its significance throughout the rest of the Old Testament. The name 'the LORD of hosts' is used to describe God as the covenant LORD who will employ all the power of

His heavenly and earthly hosts, or armies of angels and men, to relieve the affliction of His redeemed people when they have been downtrodden by their enemies for any significant period of time. This was the precise situation of the returned remnant of Jews from the Babylonian Exile in the post-exilic prophetical books. The Almighty LORD of hosts is promising to deliver them from all their enemies and to restore them fully in the far-distant future, as well as immediately by enabling them to finish rebuilding the temple. He will fulfil all His ancient, unconditional promises to the nation of Israel by sending His Messiah, Christ, to save them again, as He had originally saved them at the Exodus from Egypt. It is clear, however, that this will only happen because of the intervention of His Christ, the once-rejected Lord Jesus Christ. Accordingly, we shall now turn to consider the numerous predictions concerning Christ within the book, for they include several of the other keywords found in Zechariah's Prophecy.

6. Its Messianic Prophecies

Zechariah's Prophecy is full of Christ, a precious mine for study concerning our Lord and Saviour. George L. Robinson, a Bible scholar, called Zechariah 'the most Messianic, the most truly apocalyptic and eschatological, of all the writings of the Old Testament'. The LORD through Zechariah was encouraging His despondent and disheartened people, who had returned from the Babylonian Exile, by raising their vision to consider in glowing terms the future glories of their coming Messiah and the wonderful glory and blessing into which He will one day bring them to enjoy forever. Predictive prophecy is certainly intended to have this present stimulating practical effect upon God's people in every age. It certainly had this good effect on the discouraged remnant of Jews who had ventured to return to their former city of Jerusalem in order to re-establish the worship of their covenant LORD in a proper manner worthy of Him. Both the temple and eventually the walls of Jerusalem were rebuilt as a result of the ministry of both Haggai and Zechariah.

Zechariah's visions and predictive prophecies embrace both the first and second comings of Christ, although the emphasis is largely upon the second coming of Israel's Messiah, since the nation would reject Christ at His first coming. Certainly, Zechariah was one of the Old Testament prophets concerning whom Peter wrote that they searched diligently to understand 'what, or what manner of time the Spirit of Christ which was in them did signify, when it testified beforehand the sufferings of Christ, and the glory that should follow'; 1 Peter 1. 11. To them there appeared to be a contradiction in their messages between a suffering and a reigning Messiah which they were unable to understand. Only with the benefit of hindsight can we see clearly how these two aspects of Christ's ministry are reconciled. Christ's first coming fulfilled the predictions concerning His great sufferings, while His glorious second coming will fulfil the remainder perfectly. The Old Testament prophets were unable to see the great valley which lay between the first and second comings of Christ, since the New Testament Age of the Church of Jesus Christ was then a mystery hidden in God from previous ages prior to the formation of the one body of Christ at Pentecost by the Holy Spirit and the revelation of this mystery given later to the apostle Paul.

Turning, therefore, to consider the varied predictions concerning Christ in this short prophecy, we will first consider Him as the Man riding a red horse among the myrtle trees in a lowly hollow in chapter 1 verse 8. This Man is identified as the Angel of the LORD in verse 11, and is therefore a Christophany, or appearance of the pre-incarnate Christ in human form. This vision of Christ was intended to be an encouragement to the LORD's downtrodden people Israel, who were truly in a lowly hollow in their present experience in the world. He was standing identified with them there in all their affliction and despondency. He was not happy about the complacency of the Gentile nations around them who had subjected them to captivity any more than they were, and He was about to act on His people's behalf to help them in their weakness. It is in this context that the LORD, in verse 14, stated that He was jealous for Jerusalem and all its citizens, His own earthly people Israel. He had not finally given them up, nor ever will do so. The LORD loves and cares for Israel still, in spite of all their waywardness and disobedience in the past.

Again, in Zechariah's third vision in chapter 2 of the Man with the measuring line, who was going to measure Jerusalem, and thus claim it for God, this may again be a Christophany, a vision of the pre-incarnate Christ. Nevertheless, in chapter 3 in connection with the fourth vision, there are several different descriptions of Christ. Verse 8 speaks of Him as 'My Servant the Branch', renewing the spiritual life and fortunes of His people Israel, growing out of the felled tree stump of the house of David. Then verse 9 refers to Christ as the Stone, the foundation stone of the temple building. On it were engraved seven eyes, which symbolise His omniscience and infinite intelligence. Again, in chapter 6 verse 12, Christ is referred to as the Branch who will build the temple of the LORD. Here the reference is not so much to the second temple, which Zerubbabel was then building, but to the Millennial Temple in a day still future to us. In the same passage Christ is predicted as the future King-Priest on the restored throne of David. The two offices of king and priest will then be united in Him for the first time in Israel's history.

Zechariah's first burden in chapters 9-11 traces Christ's rejection at His first coming in humiliation and grace. In chapter 9 verse 9, the LORD through Zechariah tells Israel to rejoice greatly, because their King was going to come to them in justice and lowliness, bringing them salvation and riding on an ass, the symbol of peace, not war, and on a colt, the foal of an ass, as Matthew's Gospel chapter 21 verses 4-5 records in the fulfilment at Christ's entrance into Jerusalem before His crucifixion. Verse 10 then jumps forward in time to the beginning of Christ's Millennial reign at His second coming in glory, when He will rule in peace over the whole world. As often in Old Testament prophecy, there is no mention made of the intervening prophetic gap of the present Church Age. Chapter 11 verses 12-13 then predict Christ's betrayal for the derisory sum of thirty pieces of silver, the value of a gored slave, and how these would then be thrown into the temple in remorse by His betrayer, Judas Iscariot.

Zechariah's second burden in chapters 12-14 predicts Christ's eventual acceptance and glory at His future second coming. Chapter 12 verse 10 predicts that all Israel who survive the Great Tribulation will mourn bitterly when they see Christ returning to deliver them, because He will still be bearing the wounds which they inflicted on Him and with which they pierced Him on the cross at His first coming in grace. Then in chapter 13 verse 1, He and His precious shed blood are symbolised by the fountain of water which will be opened to cleanse Israel's sin and uncleanness, and thus make them fit for His presence. Christ's unique Deity and Humanity are referred to in chapter 13 verse 7, when the LORD calls Him both 'My Shepherd' and 'My Fellow', whom He must smite in His vicarious sacrificial death. Christ referred to this verse when He was about to be forsaken by His disciples at His arrest in the Garden of Gethsemane; see Matthew 26. 31; Mark 14. 27. By contrast, chapter 14 predicts Christ's second coming in glory and power to save Israel from all their enemies and to reign as universal King. Chapter 14 verse 5 identifies Him as 'the LORD my God', when He returns with all His saints, who include both church believers and holy angels. Verse 9 again identifies Christ as 'the LORD' who will personally be King over the whole earth.

Zechariah's predictions and descriptions of Christ are thus very wide-ranging and comprehensive of both His first and His second comings. Only Isaiah's prophecy contains a comparable revelation of prophetic truth concerning both His Person and work.

7. Its Relevance for Today's World

Here we shall consider four reasons why we should read the Prophecy of Zechariah today, whether we are believers or unbelievers. They are as follows:-

i) Because it will lead us into a deep appreciation of the LORD and His Christ.

Although the LORD's righteousness and holiness are prominent in the exhortatory passages of the book, in the vision of the cleansing of the high priest Joshua in chapter 3, and in the apocalyptic predictions concerning the future conversion of Israel in chapters 12-13 and the Millennial Kingdom in chapter 14, perhaps the major emphasis of the book is on the LORD's love and care for His afflicted and downtrodden people Israel following their bitter experience of captivity in Babylon. His positive jealousy for Israel will ensure that they will one day be fully restored to their position of blessing and glory in their own Promised Land, called here, in chapter 2 verse 12, 'the Holy Land', uniquely in Scripture. This will finally be accomplished by the direct intervention of their once-rejected Messiah, the Lord Jesus Christ, at His second coming to reign. Christ and His saving intervention then are the key to the whole plan, but the foundation for this was laid in His first coming in lowliness and grace to die for His people's sins. Zechariah's characteristic name for the LORD, 'the LORD of hosts', means that He is employing all His almighty powers, divine, angelic, and human, to achieve this end for His suffering people.

There is thus a complete and multifaceted revelation in Zechariah's Prophecy both of the character of God Himself and of the Person of His beloved Son. This should lead us all into a deeper appreciation of God the Father and His Son, more intelligent and grateful adoring worship, and more loving and diligent service.

ii) Because it reveals to us some truths more clearly than do other Bible books.

We need to read the whole Bible in order to understand the complete revelation which it contains; no part of it is redundant. We should expect, therefore, to find that Zechariah's Prophecy includes truth which is found nowhere else in the rest of Scripture so fully as here. And this is the case in at least a number of respects.

First of all, Zechariah predicts more fully than do most of the other prophets the way in which the LORD will prepare and fit His earthly people Israel for their future restoration and blessing in the coming Millennial Kingdom of Christ. According to chapter 3, He will cleanse them morally and spiritually from the filthiness of their past wicked conduct. Further, according to chapters 12-13, they will be converted and cleansed at the revelation of their rejected Messiah when He comes from heaven to deliver them from all their deadly foes. Then they will deeply mourn their past sin at His first coming. More details of the campaign of Armageddon as it will affect the Jews in Jerusalem are given in chapters 12-14 than are given in most other Scriptures. Here it is revealed that Christ will intervene only when their situation seems totally hopeless. Here it is confirmed that Christ will return to the same Mount of Olives from which the apostles saw Him ascend back into heaven. Here we learn of the earthquake which will cleave that mountain into two, so that the remnant of Jews may escape down a newly-formed valley. Here we learn that only a third of the Jews will survive the refining fires of the Great Tribulation. No other Scripture tells us this exact figure. Here, too, we learn that Jerusalem will be elevated by these earth-movements, and a great plain formed around it. Chapter 14 also reveals to us that there will be two branches to the river which will flow from the new temple, one going east to the Dead Sea, the other flowing west to the Mediterranean. Chapter 14 also reveals to us that the armies surrounding Jerusalem will be struck down by a terrible plague. Finally, the end of chapter 14 tells us valuable details about the worship which will be conducted during the Millennial Kingdom, and the penalty which will befall all nations who refuse to join in the universal worship of the LORD. There is much, therefore, in Zechariah's Prophecy which instructs us concerning the future Day of the LORD, that climactic period of the LORD's judgement and blessing, including both the Tribulation and the Millennium, which will follow the present Day of Grace after the Resurrection and Rapture of the Church. Some of its verses promise peaceful conditions during the coming kingdom of Christ and Israel's great prosperity then. These verses complement other Scriptures which also describe millennial conditions and blessings.

Secondly, other parts of the prophecy fill in the panorama of the future of Israel and other nations associated with her. All the nations which have previously been allowed to chastise Israel are here predicted to be subject to the LORD's sovereign judgement in their turn for going too far in their punishment of His erring people. The seventh vision, in chapter 5 verses 5-11, tends to confirm that the world's centre of wickedness will one day return to the land of Shinar, or Babylonia, thus supporting the view that latter-day commercial Babylon the Great of Revelation chapter 18 will be rebuilt on its old site in Babylon in Iraq. The first half of chapter 9 probably foretells the invasion of Palestine by Alexander the Great in the fourth century BC, while the first few verses of chapter 11 are thought by most commentators to predict the Roman invasions of Israel later in the first century AD as the LORD's retribution upon His people for rejecting their Messiah when He came the first time.

There is thus much in this short prophetical book which is

unique, and also there are some predictions which add to the revelation contained in other related Scriptures. We need to read Zechariah's Prophecy to discover quite a lot of valuable truth, especially concerning the history and future of the LORD's earthly people Israel.

iii) Because what the LORD said to Israel contains timeless lessons for us today.

Just because Zechariah's Prophecy largely concerns Israel and Jerusalem, rather than ourselves as members of God's heavenly people the Church, it does not mean that it is irrelevant to our lives today. Although not all Scripture is about us, it is nevertheless all intended to be read by us for our spiritual good and blessing. Israel's history is intended to teach Christian believers today many spiritual lessons, according to 1 Corinthians chapter 10 verse 11 and Romans chapter 15 verse 4. Many parallels can be drawn between God's earthly people Israel and His heavenly people, the New Testament Church, because God's moral principles of dealing with His people are the same in every age. He is the same unchangeable God throughout history.

The first, and perhaps the most important and obvious, lesson which we learn from Zechariah's Prophecy is that the earthly nation of Israel has a future, immediately very traumatic, but ultimately very glorious in the Millennial Kingdom of Christ, their true Messiah. This is so, despite their tragic rejection and crucifixion of Christ at His first coming in grace. God has not replaced Israel with the Church, as many contemporary Bible teachers and writers affirm. It is true that, according to Romans chapter 11, He has set them aside for a while during this Age of Grace in discipline for their sins, and has made His heavenly people, the Church, the present means of witness to Himself rather than Israel. However, that same chapter affirms that this is only until 'the fullness of the Gentiles be come in' (Romans 11.25), that is, after all the Church has been saved and translated to heaven at the Resurrection and Rapture. After that, all the believing remnant of Israel will be saved at the second coming of Christ in glory to deliver them from annihilation by their enemies. Then God will fulfil all the unconditional promises which He made to Abraham and David concerning their permanent possession of the Promised

Land and the continuance of the Davidic dynasty in the Person of Christ the King. He will also bring into effect His promised New Covenant of spiritual blessing and regeneration through the work of His Holy Spirit in their hearts, just as He has already done in the hearts of all believers today.

First of all, therefore, God will complete His purposes of grace for the Church at the Rapture. Then He will finish His purposes of grace and blessing for His earthly people Israel. Finally, He will achieve His original purpose for mankind, that man should rule the earth for God, during the Millennial Kingdom of Christ, the second Man who is from heaven. In short, we learn from Zechariah that, as far as Israel is concerned, 'the gifts and calling of God are without repentance'; see Romans 11. 29. The same is true of God's promises to us as members of the Church. We are totally secure in His sovereign purpose, infinite love, and unmerited grace!

The second set of spiritual lessons which we today can learn from Zechariah's Prophecy concerns the LORD's gracious ways in disciplining His wayward people, but then, upon their sincere repentance, in restoring them to blessing and favour again. We see from this prophecy the traumatic pathway which Israel will have to travel during the coming Tribulation before they are fully restored in the coming kingdom of Christ. Disobedience and departure from God are always very costly, and it usually takes many years to regain the spiritual prosperity which we at one time enjoyed before we fell into sin. For Israel this will take a few thousand years since they crucified their Messiah.

The LORD, however, has always been a God of recovery, and longs to enjoy fellowship with His people of which their sin deprived Him. In the book of Zechariah, vision after vision reassures the returned remnant of Jews that the LORD has remembered them in all their deserved affliction, and is acting, and will act, for their full and final restoration in their Promised Land during the Millennial Kingdom. We must, however, be prepared to thoroughly repent of all our sinful ways which brought God's discipline upon us, before the restoration can begin. Zechariah emphasises this in his exhortatory passages in chapters 1 and 7-8, and the full and final restoration can only come through the

LORD's direct intervention, when perhaps all seems lost for us, as it will in Israel's case according to chapters 3 and 12-14. The wonderful truth is that the LORD has, in Christ's sacrifice for sin at Calvary, made provision for our cleansing, as is depicted in Zechariah's vision of Joshua the high priest standing before the LORD wearing filthy garments, and also in the fountain of water which will be opened at the beginning of the Millennium for the cleansing of the remnant of Israel. Calvary's cross is the basis of both Israel's salvation and our own. We need to avail ourselves of its cleansing power every time we fall into sin. The LORD's ultimate objective in all His ways is to make us holy like Himself, and this is how the prophecy ends, that is, with a holy people living in peace and prosperity in His Holy Land.

iv) Because it is evident that we are now approaching the Tribulation and Second Coming of Christ of which the book speaks.

Finally, we need to read and to give heed to Zechariah's Prophecy because the time of its final fulfilment is clearly drawing near in the last days of the Church Age before the Rapture. Today, more than ever before, we are witnessing trends and events which indicate that the days of Tribulation are fast approaching, events which will only come to full fruition after the Church has departed with Christ to heaven and glory. Israel has been back in their land for quite a long time in unbelief, and their enemies around them are as eager as ever to destroy them. In fact, Israel today is the biggest sign of the coming times of Tribulation in this world, and the small nation of Israel is the main human subject of this prophetical book. Therefore, we should look up, because our own redemption, as well as that of Israel, is drawing very near. We need to prepare ourselves to meet our Lord Jesus in the air and to give account of our lives of service at the Judgement Seat. Prophecy was always intended to be intensely practical in its effect and to mould our moral character and spiritual fellowship with the Lord.

So, may this be the beneficial outcome of believers reading this book and considering Zechariah's Prophecy! Also, may unbelievers who read it be awakened to the imminent danger in which they stand without Christ, and flee to Him and the cleansing from sin which His sacrifice on Calvary procured, before they suffer the traumas of the time of Tribulation, of which this book so clearly speaks. To them the author of this commentary would like to say, that you, too, must one day meet Christ, either as your Saviour or as your Judge. He does not wish you to perish without hope, neither do you need to do so, if you will only repent of your sin and trust the Christ of whom Zechariah spoke so much and so fervently. Then you will one day become part of the future Millennial Kingdom which the prophecy predicts so much about. Maranatha! The Lord is coming! Praise His Name!

Concise Commentary on Every Chapter

CHAPTER 1

The LORD's Call to Israel to Repent and Zechariah's First and Second Night Visions concerning their Restoration

1. Zechariah's Call to Prophesy and the Key to His Message in the Meanings of His Family Names, verse 1.

Zechariah's Prophecy is dated according to the reign of a Gentile Persian emperor, rather than according to any Jewish-related date, because God's people Israel were then under His discipline. The so-called 'times of the Gentiles' (Luke 21. 24) began in 605 BC, when Nebuchadnezzar first captured Jerusalem, and will continue until the second coming of Christ. Darius ruled Persia between 521 and 486 BC, so that his second year was 520 BC, and the eighth month of that year was October-November. It was then that Zechariah was called to prophesy, as a direct message came to him from the LORD for the returned Jewish remnant in Jerusalem.

In the preceding Introduction it has been suggested that the main message of the prophecy is indicated in the respective meanings of Zechariah's family names. Zechariah means 'the LORD remembers', Berechiah means 'the LORD blesses', and Iddo means 'at His appointed time'. Putting all these thoughts together, therefore, we find that they state that the LORD is saying through Zechariah that now, after the tragedy of the Babylonian Exile, the LORD is remembering His own people Israel again, and is acting to bless and restore them to their Promised Land and His favour at His own appointed time, which the book indicates will ultimately be at Christ's second coming.

2. The LORD's Call to Israel to Repent of their Sins, verses 2-6.

The LORD's first message to the returned remnant is a call to repentance. He reminds His people that He had been very angry

31

with their ancestors because of their many sins against Him. In view of this, He pleads with them to repent of all their evil ways, so that He can change His attitude towards them to one of blessing again. Although He did intend sovereignly to bless them, they were responsible to respond to His grace by changing their behaviour towards Him. There is always in Scripture a very delicate balance between divine sovereignty and human responsibility. Three times in verse 3 the LORD uses His name 'the LORD of hosts', which contains the thought of His almighty power to deliver them from their downtrodden condition. However, the truth of the LORD's almighty power is two-edged in its implications, since it can be used either for our blessing or for our judgement, depending on our obedience or disobedience towards Him. If we wish to experience the blessing of having the LORD of hosts on our side, we need to obey Him implicitly.

In verse 4, the LORD warns His people not to be like their ancestors, who ignored and persecuted all the pre-exilic prophets who were sent to them to turn them from their evil ways. Both their ancestors and the former faithful prophets were now dead, and the judgements about which those prophets had warned them had certainly overtaken them in the Assyrian and Babylonian Exiles. God's word never returns to Him void of effect, but will always accomplish the purpose for which He gave it. We today should be warned that persistent disobedience will always lead to divine judgement. The captives of Israel and Judah had had to acknowledge that the LORD of hosts had done to them exactly what He had threatened to do, because they had not repented of their wicked ways. God is always true to His word. We should be both warned and encouraged by this truth!

3. Zechariah's First Night Vision of the Man on a Red Horse Standing among the Myrtle Trees, and the LORD's Explanation of its Meaning, verses 7-17.

There now follow eight consecutive apocalyptic night visions given in a single night to Zechariah, in order to encourage both him and the returned remnant of Jews to continue rebuilding the temple in the certain expectation that the LORD was about to restore Israel to their former place of favour and glory in their Promised Land. There is a clear progression of thought in this sequence of messages which we shall endeavour to explain as we proceed through them. Although all of them were intended to encourage the returned remnant at that time, none of them was actually fulfilled, or even partially fulfilled, in Zechariah's time. Although they did serve to inspire the returned Jews to greater efforts to finish the second temple, their fulfilment is still future to us today, awaiting Christ's second coming at the end of the Tribulation and the establishment of His Millennial Kingdom.

The date of this vision is given as the 24th Shebat, the 11th month, in Darius' second year. Shevat was the Babylonian name of this month, but it was adopted by the Jews after the Exile. This corresponds to 15th February 519 BC. This was about three months after the LORD's first message on repentance, exactly five months after work on the temple had been resumed (see Haggai 1.14-15; 2. 18), two months after Haggai had rebuked the priests and the people for delaying to build the temple (see Haggai 2. 10-17), and also two months after his prediction of the destruction of all Gentile world powers prior to the establishment of the millennial rule of Christ as the greater Zerubbabel; see Haggai 2. 20-23. It was therefore a very appropriate day on which to reveal the truths contained in these eight visions.

These eight visions were not given to Zechariah in the form of a dream while he was asleep, but while he was awake and in some form of a trance. Most of them have a standard pattern: first, some introductory words; secondly, a description of the things seen; thirdly, a question by Zechariah to an interpreting angel; fourthly, the explanation by the angel. Three of the visions are followed by summarising messages (chapter 1. 14-17; 2. 6-13; 6. 9-15), and one of them includes a message within the vision itself (chapter 4. 6-10). The angel who conversed with Zechariah was an interpreting angel, such as is found in other apocalyptic books: Daniel, Revelation, and part of Ezekiel. Angels have a large ministry in connection with future events, especially the Tribulation and judgements preceding Christ's Millennial Kingdom, which we ignore at our peril. Here the interpreting angel did not introduce the visions, but clarified their meaning to the prophet.

The first vision established the general theme of the whole

book, namely, that there was hope for the LORD's downtrodden people Israel. Despite the nation's present oppression by Gentile powers, the LORD was promising them eventual restoration and glory at the second coming of Christ to reign.

Verse 8 states that Zechariah saw in his vision a Man riding on a red horse. He was standing among myrtle trees in a hollow (AV 'bottom'), or deep valley. Behind Him there were other horses, some red, some sorrel (AV 'speckled'), that is, a mixture of other colours, and some white, and it is implied that all of them had riders on them. In reply to Zechariah's enquiry as to the identity of these horses with riders, the interpreting angel allowed the Man on the red horse to explain their meaning. The identity of this central Man in the vision is explained by verse 11, where He answers as the Angel of the LORD, that is, He is none other than the pre-incarnate Christ. Here He is identifying Himself with His despised and oppressed people Israel with a view to assuring them that He will restore them one day. Christ explained to Zechariah that the horses were agencies, clearly angelic in character, which had been sent out to patrol the whole earth, in order to assess the exact state of things there, both militarily and politically. The horses symbolise the armies, both heavenly and earthly, of the LORD of hosts supervising the affairs of the world, particularly as they affect His earthly covenant people, Israel. They were similar to the mounted messengers, or couriers, whom the Persian kings at that time used to send throughout their empire as an early kind of postal service.

The red horse Rider was clearly the central and pre-eminent figure in the vision. The riders on the other scouting horses reported their findings to Him. The colour red symbolises bloodshed and war, and speaks both of Christ as the Redeemer at His first advent, and as the Divine Warrior at His second advent, when He will judge and make war with His enemies. The myrtle trees in the deep valley are a symbol of Israel, the LORD's covenant people, as they were at that time, downtrodden and humiliated by the Gentile nations. Myrtle trees were used in connection with constructing the booths for the Feast of Tabernacles, which foreshadows the peace and rest that Israel will enjoy in the future Millennial Kingdom. Also, Isaiah referred to the myrtle tree as one of the choice plants of the Promised Land during the future Millennium; see Isaiah 41. 19; 55. 13. It reminds us of the coming glorious reign of Christ over the world, and that Israel will have a leading role to play in it. It is interesting to note here that the Hebrew name for Ahasuerus' Jewish queen Esther, namely, *Hadassah*, means 'myrtle'. The whole scene foreshadows coming millennial glory for the LORD's earthly people Israel, after their deep humiliation during the still continuing times of the Gentiles.

The riders on the other coloured horses reported back to the Angel of the LORD, the red horse Rider, that they had found that the whole earth, that is especially the whole Persian Empire, was resting quietly and complacently, despite the suffering of their oppressed subjects, the Jews. At this the pre-incarnate Christ began to intercede with His Father, the LORD of hosts, on behalf of His humiliated people Israel. Here Deity is speaking to Deity, which indicates a distinction between Persons within the Godhead, and contributes to the implicit doctrine of the Trinity in the Old Testament. He asked with great concern how long the LORD would not have mercy on Jerusalem and Judah, following His great indignation against them during their deserved Babylonian Exile. In verse 13, the LORD who answered the angel who was interpreting the vision for Zechariah may be either Person of the Godhead, that is, either the Angel of the LORD, or the LORD of hosts, that is, either God the Son or God the Father. The name is here ambiguous. However, God was about to give His servant Zechariah several good, or gracious, and comforting messages to convey to His afflicted people.

In verses 13-17, the LORD declares three main things: first, His love for Israel; secondly, His great wrath against the nations; thirdly, His promises to bless Israel. In verse 14, the LORD asserts that He is very jealous for Jerusalem and Zion. He has always ardently loved His covenant people, as a husband loves his wife, and is very jealous for her when she is wronged by others. In verse 15, He declares that, although He had been displeased with Israel for a little while, that is, during the period of the exiles, He was very angry with their oppressing Gentile neighbours, because they had aggravated Israel's affliction unreasonably harshly, and were now living at ease in carnal complacency, indifferent to

Israel's plight. Although the LORD had used them as His rod of discipline to chastise His erring people, they had not recognised this fact, but had acted only in their own interests, and attributed their success in war to their own prowess, not to the LORD, who had allowed them to achieve this. This divine anger will be fully revealed against the Gentiles in the pre-Kingdom judgements, although it has already been partially fulfilled in Old Testament times in the falls of Babylon, Medo-Persia, and Greece.

The LORD's promises to Israel are spelt out in verses 16-17. First, He promises that His presence, that is, the Shekinah glory cloud, will return to Jerusalem accompanied by His mercy. Ezekiel chapter 43 predicts the fulfilment of this promise, and his prophecy ends with the name of the LORD associated with the rebuilt city of Jerusalem, namely, 'the LORD is there'. Secondly, the LORD promises that the temple will be rebuilt. This refers primarily not to the second temple, which the Jews were then engaged in building, but to the future Millennial Temple described in Ezekiel chapters 40-48. Thirdly, likewise the city of Jerusalem will be rebuilt, which is also predicted in Ezekiel. Fourthly, He promises that the surrounding cities and towns of Israel will again overflow with wealth and prosperity. Fifthly, the LORD promises to comfort Zion after all her affliction, both deserved and undeserved, at the hands of the Gentiles. Finally, He promises to choose Jerusalem again as His chosen earthly people, which promise is repeated in chapter 2 verse 12 and in chapter 3 verse 2. Ever since Israel's rejection and crucifixion of Christ, their Messiah, at His first coming in lowliness and grace, they have been set aside as God's chief means of witness in the world in favour of the largely Gentile New Testament Church, God's heavenly people, according to Romans chapter 11. That chapter also predicts that, after the full complement of Gentiles have believed and the Church is complete and translated to heaven, God will again take up His ancient people Israel as His means of witness on the earth, and save them, both spiritually and physically, from all their enemies at His second coming in power and glory to reign.

These promises encouraged the Jews of that time to finish building the second temple and, later, the city of Jerusalem, although in their full meaning they will not be finally fulfilled before the beginning of the future Millennial Kingdom. The themes of the LORD's anger against the Gentile nations around them, and the predictions of Israel's future blessing, continue in the next two visions, to which we now turn.

4. Zechariah's Second Night Vision of the Four Horns and the Four Craftsmen/Carpenters, and the LORD's Explanation of its Meaning, verses 18-21.

This second vision shows the LORD's judgement on the nations who have afflicted Israel down the centuries, while the third vision shows His blessing in prospering Israel in their land. The vision of the four horns and four craftsmen (AV 'carpenters'), that is, artisans, or smiths (RV), since they work in metal, stone, or wood, shows how the LORD will execute His anger on the oppressing Gentile nations. As the LORD had once said through Isaiah concerning 'the servants of the LORD', that is, the faithful remnant of Israel, 'No weapon that is formed against thee shall prosper; and every tongue that shall rise against thee in judgment thou shalt condemn'; Isaiah 54. 17. God has always, and will always, vindicate and deliver a remnant of Israel from all their oppressing enemies.

When Zechariah looked up again in his trance, he saw a vision of four horns. To his enquiry to the interpreting angel concerning their identity, the latter replied that they represented the horns which have scattered Judah, Israel, and Jerusalem. No further explanation is given concerning their identity. Since horns represent the power of particular kingdoms, or empires, we are left to deduce which kingdoms or empires are meant by these symbols. Since all the eight night visions predict events right up to the establishment of the Millennial Kingdom, the four horns could symbolise the four great world empires who have ruled during the times of the Gentiles, namely, Babylon, Medo-Persia, Greece, and Rome. Zechariah could have derived this from the Prophecy of Daniel, chapters 2 and 7. However, since Israel as well as Judah is mentioned here, some commentators see in the four horns a reference to Assyria, Egypt, Babylon, and Medo-Persia. Still others suggest the Gentile nations which immediately surrounded Israel and Judah. Again, some suggest that the number four, which usually in Scripture represents universality, may indicate that the vision concerns all Gentile powers who ever have tried to oppose and destroy Israel down the centuries until the establishment of Christ's kingdom on earth.

When the LORD further showed Zechariah four craftsmen, or smiths, He explained to him that these men represented agencies of judgement which would arise in the world to terrify and cast down the four horns of the Gentiles which have used their power to scatter Israel. The precise identity of these craftsmen clearly depends on the identity of the horns. If the horns represent the four world empires of Daniel's visions, then the four craftsmen would represent the kingdoms which succeeded each of these empires and destroyed their predecessor's empire. Thus we could say that Medo-Persia destroyed Babylon, Greece destroyed Medo-Persia, Rome destroyed Greece, and Christ in His ultimate Messianic kingdom will destroy the Revived Roman Empire under the Beast of Revelation chapter 13. Certainly the vision embraces the whole time up to the Millennial Kingdom. It could, therefore, be maintained that, since the four craftsmen in the vision apparently all destroy the four horns at one and the same time, it is a prophecy which primarily anticipates the end of the times of the Gentiles, when all the powerful nations of the world will besiege Israel and Jerusalem at the crisis of Armageddon, intending to completely annihilate the LORD's earthly people. We know from chapter 14 of this prophecy, as also from Psalm 2, Joel chapter 3, and Revelation chapter 19, that the LORD in the Person of Jesus Christ at His second coming will intervene then to destroy all the attacking nations and to save His people Israel. Perhaps we are also meant to understand the abiding truth that, in any and every age of human history, God will raise up instruments of judgement to deliver His chosen people Israel from all their enemies. This is how He proves His jealousy for them. Whatever may be the correct primary interpretation of this second vision, it would certainly have encouraged the returned remnant of Jews after the Babylonian Exile to continue the work of building the second temple.

CHAPTER 2

Zechariah's Third Night Vision concerning the Man with the Measuring Line, Promising the Protection and Restoration of Future Jerusalem

1. The People Mentioned in the Vision, verses 1-4a.

The purpose of this vision is to reassure the returned remnant of Jews from Babylon in Zechariah's day concerning the successful material restoration of Jerusalem, and also, in its wider meaning, to predict a still greater fulfilment in its yet future restoration during Christ's Millennial Kingdom. If the message of Zechariah's second vision had been primarily negative, assuring the defeat of all Israel's enemies, the message of his third vision is wholly positive, promising God's chosen people protection and material prosperity in their Promised Land again.

When Zechariah looks up again, after the second vision had departed, he sees a mysterious Man holding a measuring line in His hand going out to measure the length and breadth of Jerusalem, like a surveyor. The exact identity of this Man is not stated, but may perhaps be deduced from the context of the previous visions, especially the first one. Since He cannot be equated with either the interpreting angel mentioned in verse 3, or the 'young man' of verse 4, who must be Zechariah himself, at that time (520-519 BC) still evidently quite young, He is probably best identified with the Angel of the LORD of chapter 1, that is, the pre-incarnate Christ. In chapter 6 verse 12, Christ is called, in a clearly Messianic passage, 'the Man, whose name is THE BRANCH'. Therefore, there is no difficulty in holding that 'the Man' here is Christ Himself. Ezekiel also speaks of Him as 'a Man whose appearance was like...bronze, with a measuring rod in His hand'; Ezekiel 40. 2-3 (NASB). The pre-incarnate Christ had always delighted to be with the sons of men, according to Proverbs chapter 8 verse 31, and had appeared in various forms to a few of His servants in what are often called Christophanies. Here Christ is probably to be distinguished from the 'another angel' of verse 3, who went out to meet the interpreting angel and instructed him what to say to Zechariah in the following verses. Christ is the divine Surveyor of future Jerusalem, and there are two angels subordinate to Him involved in the communication of this vision to Zechariah.

2. The LORD's Promises concerning Future Jerusalem, verses 4b-13.

This third vision was full of good news for Zechariah and his contemporaries, who were struggling to finish rebuilding a ruined city and its temple. In its ultimate fulfilment, however, it anticipates a day still future to us now, when Israel and Jerusalem will be finally restored in the Millennial Kingdom. Here there are at least five precious promises for Israel to treasure for their encouragement. Note that the angel's message is addressed first to Zechariah as the 'young man' (verses 4-5), then to Israel (verses 6-12), and finally to all mankind (AV 'all flesh') (verse 13).

The first promise, given in verse 4, is that Jerusalem would enjoy a prosperous expansion of its boundaries. Not only would Jerusalem be inhabited, but it would expand into open, unprotected countryside outside the city itself and embrace many towns in its suburbs. Such would be its expansion in terms of both human and animal occupation. This expansion awaits the Millennial Kingdom, when Jerusalem will become the world's capital, will occupy a larger area than it does now, and will be elevated above its present altitude; see Isaiah 2. 2-3; 49. 19-20.

The second promise, given in verse 5, is that Jerusalem will experience special divine protection and glory. The LORD promised to be a wall of fire round about her, and the glory in the midst of her. He will be much more than a wall of protection from external enemies negatively; rather, in positive blessing He will dwell in their midst again in the Shekinah glory cloud, which will return to the Millennial Temple; see Ezekiel 43. 1-7.

In verses 6-7, the third promise is that Israel will be regathered to her Promised Land and restored. Their attention is arrested by the two-fold onomatopoeic exclamation 'Ho!' They are warned to flee from the land of the north, that is, Babylon, which had previously attacked Israel from the north. While this initially refers to the return from the Babylonian Exile, it also foreshadows the call in a future day to inhabitants of Babylon the Great to come out of that city before it is destroyed by God; see Revelation 18. 4-8. Similarly, the return from the exile was only a partial fulfilment of the promise of the regathering of Israel. The full and final regathering will take place at the beginning of the Millennial Kingdom. Israel today has been scattered throughout the Gentile nations of the world like the four winds of heaven in divine discipline. Here Israel is urged to deliver themselves from further judgement by escaping from Babylon while they could.

In verses 8-9, the LORD's fourth promise to His people is that the nations which had been plundering and oppressing them would be judged and punished. He prefaces His promise with His name 'the LORD of hosts', which means that He is promising to exert His almighty power in heaven and earth to deliver His poor oppressed people. The phrase 'after the glory hath He sent Me unto the nations which spoiled you' is somewhat difficult to understand clearly. The first phrase is literally 'after glory', rather than 'after the glory' and probably means that the LORD will be glorified upon the nations by judging them. As F.A. Tatford says: 'the ...probable significance is that the action taken was a demonstration of God's glory or a vindication of it'. He quotes David Baron, who says that 'it means to vindicate and to display the glory of God, first in the judgements which He is to inflict on the nations who have oppressed Israel, and then in the exhibition of His grace in the deliverance and salvation of His own people'. The reference in the word 'Me' in verse 8 must be to Christ, whom the LORD will send to judge and deliver Israel at His second coming. Then the LORD reassures Israel that He will deliver them because they are 'the apple of His eye', most dear and precious to Him. No-one can touch, or harm, Israel with impunity. The LORD will shake, or brandish, His hand over Israel as their powerful Champion, in order to confound their enemies, who will become plunder for Israel and their servants in the coming kingdom. Thus Israel would know that the LORD of hosts had sent Christ, the Angel of the LORD, who is referred to again here as 'Me'. The divine Christ will be the Deliverer of Israel, who will experience a complete reversal of their fortunes in the Millennial Kingdom.

In verses 10-12, the fifth promise is that the LORD will come to dwell in the midst of Israel in Jerusalem, and that in the coming Day of the LORD many nations will join themselves to the LORD in obedient faith and also become His people. Israel will then know what she previously refused to believe, that is, that it was the LORD of hosts, the God of Israel, who had sent Christ to them. Although many other nations will be converted then and be blessed alongside Israel, Judah will still be the LORD's special inheritance. Then, also, the land of Israel will become truly 'the Holy Land', which phrase occurs only here in the Scriptures. Previously it had not been characterised by holiness at all, but after the cleansing and conversion of Israel, it will live up to its name. Again the LORD asserts that then He will choose Jerusalem once more, after the nation had been set aside during the times of the Gentiles and the whole of the Church Age. Israel has a future, immediately traumatic, but ultimately very glorious.

Finally, in verse 13, the LORD commands all mankind to be silent as He will come from His holy dwelling-place in heaven, in the Person of Christ His Messiah, to judge the world, to deliver His people Israel, and to establish His everlasting kingdom in the earth. He will be roused into decisive action by the wickedness of mankind and the need of His people Israel. This verse thus clearly predicts the second coming of Christ. Help and restoration are on the way for Israel. How much more should Christians today be anticipating the prior imminent coming of their Heavenly Bridegroom at the Resurrection and Rapture of the Church! Maranatha! The Lord is coming for us soon!

CHAPTER 3

Zechariah's Fourth Night Vision of the Cleansing of Joshua, the High Priest, from the Defilement of Sin as the Prerequisite for the Restoration of Israel to their Role in the World

1. Joshua's Cleansing from Iniquity Effected, verses 1-5.

In view of the wonderful material blessings which are in store for Israel, as revealed in the previous visions, the question arises as to how an absolutely holy God can possibly accomplish these plans with such a sinful and defiled nation as Israel had so far proved themselves to be. The answer which this prophecy gives is that He can do so on the basis of the redemptive work of Christ on Calvary, and after they have repented and believed in Him at His second coming. Then at last Israel will give up trying to establish their own righteousness (Romans 10. 3), and submit themselves to the righteousness of God in Christ by faith alone; Romans 3. 22. This fourth vision is thus a clear foreshadowing of the future spiritual conversion of Israel, when Christ will be accepted at His second coming; see chapter 12. Then all their blessings will begin, and the way will be made open for them to fulfil their divinely-appointed role of witness in the world, as we shall see in chapter 4.

Verse 1 states that the interpreting angel then showed Zechariah Joshua the high priest standing before the Angel of the LORD, who is identified as 'the LORD' in verse 2, to serve Him in his priestly capacity with Satan also standing there at his right side to be his adversary, as if Joshua was in court before the LORD's judgement throne. Joshua is clearly standing there as the representative of his people Israel, since the LORD in verse 2 rebukes Satan, not on the basis of His personal choice of Joshua, but on the basis of His divine choice of Jerusalem, that is, all Israel. Israel's sins had given a place of advantage to Satan to accuse them before the LORD. Joshua made no attempt to answer Satan's charges against his nation, since they were quite true. But the LORD answered for him with a double rebuke of Israel's adversary, which only He is qualified to administer to His former anointed cherub. We dare not rebuke Satan; neither did the archangel Michael in Jude verse 9. The basis of the LORD's rebuke was His gracious choice of Jerusalem, His unmerited favour towards Israel, and nothing else. Here we learn that, if God is for us, no-one can effectively stand against us as His chosen people today, as Israel was then; see Romans chapter 8 verse 31. Otherwise, none of us could ever have been saved. Our salvation and standing before God are all the result of His sovereign electing grace; like Israel, we are only brands plucked from the fires of hell. The disobedient Jews had just returned from the fires of exile in Babylon by the LORD's sovereign permission, having borne His wrath there for a while as punishment for their sins, but now the LORD was reaffirming His purpose to save His earthly people and to recommission them in His service. He would not allow His adversary to frustrate that purpose of grace and mercy now.

Then, in verse 3, Zechariah noticed that Joshua, Israel's representative, was standing before the Angel of the LORD, the pre-incarnate Christ, wearing filthy (literally 'excrement soiled') garments, not clean priestly garments. Not only was Israel guilty before the LORD's judgement bar, but also utterly defiled in character and unfit for His presence. Now, however, the LORD acts in pure, undeserved grace, and commands the angelic attendants in the vision to take away the filthy garments from Joshua, and to clothe him instead with 'festal robes' (NASB). This beautifully illustrates the means by which all sinners are ever justified, clothed with the righteousness of God in Christ, forgiven, and cleansed by God on the basis of the death of Christ for our sins. The nation of Israel will come nationally into the good of this salvation when they are converted at the second coming of Christ; see chapters 12-13. Christians today have come into the good of this salvation long before Israel will.

In verse 5, we find that Zechariah was so carried away with enthusiasm when he saw the cleansing and clothing of the high priest, whom he probably understood to represent his people in the future, that he interrupted the proceedings to request that the angelic attendants in his vision set a clean turban (AV 'fair mitre') on Joshua's head, and also clothe him with the high-priestly garments of glory and beauty. The turban of fine linen bore on its front a gold plate, on which were engraved the words 'Holiness to the LORD'; Exodus 28.36. It indicated that Joshua was now morally and spiritually fit to minister to the LORD, as Israel will minister to Him as a nation of priests during the Millennial Kingdom. The Angel of the LORD was standing beside Zechariah while he made this interjection, approving of his well-meaning action. The LORD is gracious and encouraging towards those who act spontaneously with similar godly enthusiasm.

2. *The LORD'S Charge to Joshua, verses 6-7.*

The Angel of the LORD, that is, the pre-incarnate Christ, now gives to Joshua a solemn admonition to walk in the ways of the LORD of hosts who had just cleansed him and made him fit to engage in fellowship with, and service for, Him again; the recipients of God's unmerited grace and favour are never exempt from obedience and faithfulness to His word. If the nation of Israel, who are here represented by Joshua their high priest, were to keep the LORD's charge, or commandment, then both he and they would be permitted to exercise priestly judgement in the rebuilt temple, which is the LORD's house, or dwelling-place, and also to enjoy other spiritual privileges along with the attending angels, who were present in this vision. With gracious privilege always goes solemn responsibility.

3. *The Prophetic Significance of the Vision concerning Christ and Israel Explained, verses 8-10.*

Now, in verses 8-10, there follows a remarkable Messianic passage, since the LORD affirms that both Joshua the high priest of Israel and all his fellow-priests, who were sitting before him, are symbolic figures (literally 'men of sign') who in their persons foreshadowed future events which would one day affect their whole nation of Israel for decisive good and blessing. They portray in their priestly ministries the priestly ministry of Israel in the yet future day of their cleansing and conversion. The question arises as to how Israel will be redeemed and restored to her privilege as a high-priestly nation. Who will achieve this great transformation in the nation's fortunes? The answer given here is that the Messiah, Christ, will effect this change. He will do so, first of all, under the figure of the LORD's Servant, who will fulfil all God's will perfectly, unlike Israel in the past, also under the figure of the BRANCH, the restorer of the life and fortunes of the dynasty of David, which had been felled in divine discipline to a mere stump by the Babylonian Exile. The pre-exilic prophets Isaiah and Jeremiah had previously referred to Christ in this way; see Isaiah 4. 2; 11. 1; Jeremiah 23. 5; 33. 15. Zechariah again speaks of Christ, the unique Priest-King, as the BRANCH in chapter 6 verses 12-13.

Secondly, in verse 9, Christ is presented as 'the stone', as so often throughout Scripture in both Testaments. As such He is the foundation upon whom the fulfilment of all God's purposes of grace and judgement are based as a result of His death and resurrection; see Genesis 49. 24; Psalm 118. 22; Isaiah 28. 16; Daniel 2. 45; Matthew 21. 42; Acts 4. 11; 1 Peter 2. 6. In Zechariah's vision the LORD said that this stone had seven eyes, which elsewhere represent divine omniscience to judge or to bless. Christ as the Lamb in the midst of the throne in Revelation chapter 5 verse 6 has seven eyes, which are there said to be the 'seven Spirits of God sent forth into all the earth', the Holy Spirit in all His divine fullness. This stone is further said to bear an inscription, like a carved precious gemstone, enhancing its beauty. This may foreshadow the marks which Christ suffered at Calvary, but which qualified Him to be both Israel's and our Saviour. This would one day be the only way in which the LORD of hosts would solve the problem of sin in the universe, and specifically remove the iniquity of the land of Israel in one day, that is, when He comes again in glory and power to judge and reign; see chapters 12-13. The climactic day referred to is Israel's great future Day of Atonement, when the rituals and sacrifices of the Old Testament Day of Atonement of Leviticus chapter 23 will all be fulfilled. Then the remnant of the nation of Israel will look on the once-crucified, but now resurrected and glorified, Saviour and deeply mourn their tragic sin against Him at His first coming in humiliation. Their national conversion and regeneration will immediately take place then, and they will be ready at last to enter Christ's glorious kingdom on earth.

Thirdly, verse 10 confirms these truths by affirming that in that Day of the LORD, the beginning of the Millennial Kingdom, every man will dwell in peace and prosperity, both materially and spiritually, under his own vine and fig tree, a picture of millennial conditions throughout the earth. The imagery is taken from King Solomon's reign, which was a foreshadowing of Christ's future Millennial Kingdom as the Greater than Solomon; see 1 Kings 4. 24-25; Micah 4. 4. Thus will the LORD through Christ solve Israel's many problems caused by their sins against Him throughout history, and so at last prepare them to fulfil their divinely-appointed role for Him in the world, as we shall see in chapter 4.

CHAPTER 4

Zechariah's Fifth Night Vision of the Golden Lampstand and the Two Olive Trees, Symbolising Israel's Role as the LORD's Witness in the World in the Power of the Holy Spirit through Joshua the High Priest and Zerubbabel the Governor

Israel's cleansing from sin and restoration to her divine calling as a high-priestly nation, set out in Zechariah's fourth vision, will be the necessary preparation for her worldwide ministry of witness to her LORD during the Millennial Kingdom of Christ the Priest-King, which is portrayed in this fifth vision. The two visions teach the spiritual order of salvation before service. There is here also a contemporary message of encouragement for Zerubbabel in his building of the second temple.

1. The Prophetic Symbolism of the Vision Outlined, verses 1-5.

At this point in the sequence of visions the interpreting angel roused Zechariah from his trance like a man wakened from sleep. Perhaps the prophet was overcome by the wonder of the foregoing visions concerning the future of his people Israel, as was Daniel in his prophetic revelations (Daniel 10. 9), and also as were Peter, James, and John on the Mount of Transfiguration; Luke 9. 32. When the angel asked Zechariah what he saw, the prophet replied that he saw a lampstand made all of gold with a bowl on the top of it, seven lamps on the lampstand with seven pipes feeding into each of the seven lamps, and two olive trees, one on either side of the lampstand feeding oil into the bowl above the lampstand. Thus this lampstand was very different in its construction from the golden lampstand in the tabernacle. There were evidently forty-nine pipes feeding the seven lamps, which meant that the supply of oil to the lamps here was far greater than the supply given to the tabernacle lampstand. Also, the maintenance of its light depended entirely upon the supernatural supply of oil from above via the golden bowl, whereas the tabernacle lampstand was maintained by the human agency of the Levitical priests. Zechariah asked the interpreting angel what the two olive trees represented. He seemed surprised that Zechariah did not know. The prophet confessed his ignorance, and was not fully answered until later in the vision, in verse 14. Instead, the angel first gave a message of encouragement to Zerubbabel based on the vision of the lampstand.

2. The Meaning of the Vision for Zerubbabel Explained, verses 6-10.

The angel explained that the vision contained a word of the LORD, a divine revelation, to Zerubbabel concerning the rebuilding of the temple, in which he was then engaged amid many difficulties and much opposition. Although the vision in its full meaning foreshadows the witness of Israel during Christ's Millennial Kingdom, it nevertheless was very relevant also to the small remnant of Jews who had returned under Zerubbabel, for whom there was a partial fulfilment. In verse 6, the angel revealed that the main message of the vision was that the LORD's work of finishing the rebuilding of the second temple would only be accomplished by the supernatural and abundant supply of the power of the Holy Spirit, who is always signified by the symbol of oil in Scripture. No human might or power could do this, but with the aid of the Spirit of God all things are possible. No great mountain of opposition from their enemies, nor the natural weakness and apathy of the returned remnant, would prevent the work from being completed now. This opposing mountain would be levelled to become a plain before Zerubbabel, so that he would soon be able to put the capstone on the top of the temple structure amid shouts of rejoicing as the people would see how lovely and graceful the finished building looked.

Zechariah was then inspired by a further revelation from the LORD to reassure the returned remnant that, just as Zerubbabel had originally laid the foundation of the new house of God with his own hands, so surely his hands would finish it soon. This would be proof that the LORD had sent His Angel, who is here the pre-incarnate Christ, to give this message through Zechariah to His despised people. They need not despise the present day of apparently small things by comparison with the past day of the building of Solomon's much larger and more magnificent temple. They would rejoice when they saw the plumb-line again in Zerubbabel's hands as he superintended the building work. The reference in verse 10 to 'these seven' is to the omniscient eyes of the LORD which range throughout the whole earth overseeing His divine work and empowering its accomplishment. Zerubbabel here is really a type of the future Zerubbabel, as he is presented in Haggai's prophecy chapter 2 verses 20-23, who is Christ, the Messiah Himself, for it will be Christ who will build the Millennial Temple (Ezekiel chapters 40-42), which will be the full and final fulfilment of the meaning of this vision.

The abiding message of Zechariah's fifth vision is that all spiritual work requires the abundant supply of the power of the Holy Spirit for its successful accomplishment and outcome. In the future Millennial Kingdom there will be a superabundant supply of the Holy Spirit's power to accomplish all God's purposes of grace and judgement through Christ. The message for us today is that, unless we have the Holy Spirit's divine enabling and empowering, nothing will be achieved at all in the face of all the difficulties which the enemy of our souls puts in our way as we serve the LORD. We cannot successfully serve Him in our own strength. May we constantly learn this essential lesson in our various present ministries!

3. The Interpretation of the Two Olive Trees Given, verses 11-14.

Now Zechariah returns to the subject of the identity of the two olive trees on either side of the golden bowl over the lampstand, and again asks the interpreting angel for an explanation both of them and of the two golden pipes, or branches (literally 'ears'), which emptied the oil from the two olive trees into the bowl. Again, the angel seemed surprised that Zechariah did not understand their significance, but now he does explain their meaning, although in a rather veiled way. He said that they represented the 'two anointed ones', literally 'sons of oil', who stand by the sovereign Lord of the whole earth to supply power to accomplish His work. In the immediate context of this prophecy, they clearly refer primarily to Joshua the high priest and Zerubbabel the governor of Judah, who had both been anointed for their offices, but in the prophecy's full and final fulfilment they probably refer to Christ in His future role during the Millennial Kingdom as the divine Priest-King upon His throne; for the phrase 'the Lord of the whole earth' has a future millennial significance. Also, as Revelation chapter 11 verses 3-6 explains, another partial fulfilment of this prophetic vision of the two olive trees is to be found in the lives and supernatural ministry of the two witnesses who will stand for God during the future Tribulation period. We see, therefore, that there are, and will be, several partial fulfilments of the meaning of this vision, as well as a meaning for the time of the returned remnant, and a final fulfilment in the worldwide witness of Israel during the future kingdom of Christ. How full of significance every part of Scripture is for all of us, the LORD's servants! What a warning and an encouragement is found here in this chapter! Without the power and working of the Holy Spirit Himself we can achieve absolutely nothing worthwhile for God!

CHAPTER 5

Zechariah's Sixth and Seventh Night Visions: First, that of the Flying Scroll which Judges the Sins of All Transgressors in the World; Secondly, that of the Woman inside the Large Measuring Basket, which is Removed to the Land of Babylonia, Symbolising the Removal of Commercial and Religious Wickedness from the Earth Prior to the Millennial Kingdom

Here the sequence of visions takes a definite turn from a comforting and encouraging tone to one of judgement of all iniquity in view of the coming kingdom of Christ. God will not tolerate any sin in either His own people Israel or in any of the inhabitants of His world during the Millennial Kingdom. Both in preparation for that kingdom age, and during its continuance, transgressors will be dealt with severely under Christ's rule with a rod of iron. Conditions of life then will be somewhat different from those which pertain at present during the Age of Grace and the Gospel, when God is waiting patiently for mankind to repent and trust Him, and is not yet judging sin immediately. Accordingly, the three remaining visions all deal with the theme of judgement: first upon Israel individually (chapter 5. 1-4); then on Israel nationally (chapter 5. 5-11); finally on all nations internationally (chapter 6. 1-8).

1. The Vision of the Flying Scroll Described and Explained, verses 1-4.

When Zechariah lifted up his eyes again in his trance, he saw a flying roll, or scroll, completely unwound and floating in the air like a large sheet. It contained writing on both sides, like the two tables of the Mosaic Law, of which it is reminiscent. In verse 2, the size of the scroll is given, namely, twenty cubits long by ten cubits wide, that is, about thirty feet long by fifteen feet wide. This was the exact size of the wilderness tabernacle. The inference is that the judgements coming from the scroll were in accordance with the holiness of the LORD's dwelling-place in the midst of His people Israel. The measurements are also identical with those of the porch of Solomon's Temple. This might imply that the threatened judgement would begin at the house of God, but this is a less likely interpretation.

Verse 3 states that this scroll is a symbol of God's curse against sinners, especially those in Israel, for breaking the Ten Commandments. Since the curse is said to cover the whole earth, it will affect all sinners, both before the establishment of the Millennial Kingdom, and during its course. It signifies the punishment which will fall on all law-breakers. Compare Revelation chapters 5 verses 1-9 and 10 verses 1-11 for a similar scroll or little book which will unleash God's judgements upon sinners prior to the setting up of Christ's kingdom. The two commandments which are cited as being broken are the two middle commandments of the two tables of the law, namely, the eighth against stealing and the third against swearing falsely by the LORD's name. They are probably intended to represent all the others. All who break these commandments will be cut off, that is, executed summarily. This will apply both during the Tribulation and during the course of the kingdom on earth; for, although at the beginning of the kingdom all unsaved sinners will be killed and not enter the millennium, children who are born from converted parents will not all believe the gospel and be saved, but will sometimes lapse into sinful ways. Even the saved may occasionally lapse into sin. Such lapses will be severely punished. Verse 4, therefore, predicts the severity of the judgement for sins committed which will be applied then. The whole house of the habitual thief and the persistent perjurer will be completely destroyed until it is an utter ruin.

Thus this vision goes beyond the circumstances of Zechariah's day and indicates for the Israel of the future that, when Christ comes in power and glory to reign, God is going to pour out His judgement on the whole world and remove every sinner from the land. The Age of Grace will be over, and Christ will rule with a rod of iron, as several Scriptures predict; see Psalm 2. 9-12; Revelation 12. 5; 19. 15. Unbelieving sinners today are warned to be reconciled to God through Christ now while there is time to repent and trust Him as Saviour, before they meet Him as their rightful Judge!

2. *The Vision of the Woman in the Ephah Described and Explained, verses 5-11.*

Zechariah's seventh vision, which the interpreting angel now directed him to consider, was of a woman sitting inside an ephah, that is, a large measuring basket, or barrel, which was also in flight. Since this would normally be too small a container to hold a woman, the ephah was apparently greatly enlarged in the vision for emphasis, as the flying scroll had been in the previous vision. The angel then explained the meaning of the ephah at the end of verse 6, but the Hebrew text here is somewhat uncertain. The AV, following the Massoretic Text, translates it as follows: 'This is their resemblance (literally, 'their eye or appearance') through all the earth', that is, the Jewish people's resemblance, or likeness, in all the land of Israel. In Babylon the exiled Jews had become characterised by materialism and were covetous for commercial gain. This must be the meaning of the passage, since verse 8 identifies the woman in the ephah as 'wickedness'. The Septuagint and Syriac translate the end of verse 6 as follows: 'This is the iniquity of the people', which is the less difficult reading to understand in the context of verse 8, but because it is the easier reading to understand, it is less likely to have been the original reading.

Verse 7 reveals that the woman, who represented commercial wickedness, was held down inside the ephah by a heavy lid of a talent of lead. The interpreting angel made sure that the woman was securely confined in the ephah, in order that she might be removed from the land of Israel altogether. The significance of the vision for the Jews in Zechariah's time was that wickedness must be removed from their country in preparation for its final judgement elsewhere. A woman in Scripture is sometimes used as a symbol of spiritual evil. Other instances are: the woman in Matthew chapter 13 verse 33, who hid leaven in meal until it was all leavened; 'that woman Jezebel, who calleth herself a prophetess' in Revelation chapter 2 verse 20, but taught the saints to sin; lastly, and most significantly here, the woman of Revelation chapter 17 verses 3-17, the great harlot, Babylon the Great, the pinnacle of religious evil in the Tribulation, who will ride the Beast for a time. Religious and commercial evil are evidently closely connected. Zechariah was seeing in symbolical form the Satanic world system at the time when it is about to be removed both from God's people, Israel, and then from all earth's inhabitants.

In verse 9, Zechariah now saw two other, unidentified, women approaching with the power of the wind in their wings, which resembled those of a stork, an unclean bird. These women probably represent evil demonic forces, albeit under God's sovereign permissive control. They lifted up the ephah containing the woman called 'wickedness' into mid-air. When the prophet asked the angel where they were intending to transport the ephah, he said that they were going to build it a house in the land of Shinar, which is Babylonia. There it would become established firmly on its base, evidently as an idolatrous image. Babylon was the place where the Jews had recently been exiled, but it is also the site of both ancient and future idolatry and rebellion against God; see Genesis 11. 2; Revelation 17-18. We are seeing here in symbolical form the consummation of human wickedness in Babylon the Great, and it is implied that, when it appears in its final form in the Tribulation in the Middle East in the idolatrous worship of the image of the Beast, it will be summarily judged there, as Revelation records in the two chapters referred to above. Thus this vision in its meaning goes far beyond Zechariah's day and the return of the Jews from the Babylonian Exile, and it anticipates the idolatry and commercial wickedness of the end times, which other Scriptures also clearly predict. It supports the increasingly widely held view among contemporary Bible students that Babylon will be rebuilt on its original site, and also confirms the fact that, before Christ can reign in righteousness and peace in His Millennial Kingdom, all unbelieving sinners and all iniquity must be judged and removed from the world.

Zechariah's Eighth Vision of the Four War Chariots, Symbolising the LORD's Worldwide Judgement, followed by the Crowning of Joshua the High Priest, Symbolising Christ as the Future Millennial King-Priest

This last vision of the four chariots is connected with the first vision in the series, which also concerned a number of horses. In the first vision the horses' riders were sent to find out the attitude of the nations of the earth towards the LORD's people Israel in captivity. There the nations were found to be completely complacent about the oppressed condition in which Israel was found. The LORD therefore determined to throw the nations into confusion, in order that they might restore Israel to their land. This is not clearly stated here, but it is in Haggai's prophecy chapter 2 verses 6-7 and 20-22. The last vision now assumes that this shaking has taken place, and the four war chariots and their riders are in the process of executing the LORD's judgements on the nations around Israel for their oppression of His people. This chapter in its ultimate reference, therefore, portrays to us the international aspect of the LORD's still future judgements prior to the setting up of Christ's Millennial Kingdom. It goes far beyond the events of Zechariah's time, although it certainly served the purpose of reassuring the returned remnant that the LORD would see that justice would be executed upon the nations eventually.

1. The Vision of the Four Chariots Described, verses 1-3.

As in chapter 5 verse 1, Zechariah now turned, lifted up his eyes, and looked at the next, the last, vision of that eventful night of revelation. When he did this, he saw four war chariots coming out from between two mountains which were made of bronze (AV 'brass'). This whole scene speaks of divine judgement being executed on the world, since the symbols 'chariots' and 'bronze' in Scripture are both used in connection with God's judgement upon mankind. The two mountains are not identified, so that we cannot be certain that they are intended to represent any particular mountains. Some commentators have suggested that, since the definite article is included in the text, which reads, 'the two mountains', they could refer to Mount Zion and Mount Olivet. Joel chapter 3 verse 2 mentions the valley of Jehoshaphat in connection with the Lord's judgement of the nations at the second coming, but not a mountain. Zechariah chapter 14 verse 4 mentions the Mount of Olives, but does not directly refer to a judgement of the nations then. Therefore, we cannot be dogmatic about this reference to 'the two mountains'. The four war chariots pulled by differently coloured horses speak of the universality of divine judgement which will go in all directions throughout the world at that time. The four horses are clearly similar to the four horsemen of Revelation chapter 6 verses 1-8, who also appear in the context of the judgement of mankind on earth. The red horses of the first chariot symbolise war and bloodshed; compare Revelation 6. 4. The black horses of the second chariot symbolise famine and death; compare Revelation 6. 5-6. The white horses of the third chariot symbolise victory; compare Revelation 6. 2. The grizzled, or dappled, and bay, or strong, steeds of the fourth chariot are similar to the pale horse of Revelation chapter 6 verse 8, which symbolises wholesale death from many causes besides war, such as pestilence and plague.

2. The Explanation of the Vision Given, verses 4-8.

When Zechariah asked the interpreting angel for an explanation of the four war chariots and horses, the angel replied that they represented the four angelic spirits who were standing in attendance on God as the sovereign Lord of the whole earth ready to execute His will. The phrase 'the Lord of the whole earth' anticipates His universal sovereignty during the future Millennial Kingdom, for which these angelic agencies are preparing the way by judging all the rebellious opposing empires which will have ruled on earth before that time. The horses thus symbolise particular judgements, while the war chariots symbolise the angelic beings who execute those judgements. Verse 6 explains that the black horses were going to judge the north country, from which Israel's greatest enemies always came, namely, the Assyrians, Babylonians, Seleucid Greeks, and Romans. The white horses were sent after them. Meanwhile the dappled horses went towards the south country, where Israel's first oppressor Egypt lay. Also, the strong bay steeds went out to roam to and fro throughout the whole world to execute the LORD's judgements. Note that the red horses are not mentioned in verses 6-7, perhaps surprisingly. Some commentators have therefore equated them with the strong steeds of verse 7, but it is not possible to be certain about this identification. What is clear is that the various angelic agencies will be sent out before the establishment of Christ's Millennial Kingdom to judge all opposition to the LORD in whatever part of the world it will be found. In verse 8, the interpreting angel, speaking for the LORD here, declares that now that these judgements have taken place, especially in the north country of Babylonia, His spirit is appeased, since justice has at last been done, and His people Israel will have been relieved from their oppression by the various Gentile kingdoms. In particular, before the kingdom is set up, Babylon will be judged finally, as Revelation chapters 17-18 confirms. This eighth vision given to Zechariah undoubtedly encouraged his contemporaries, who were struggling to rebuild the temple amidst much opposition from the Gentile kingdoms, especially from those in the north country of Babylonia.

Thus, the whole panorama of the eight visions not only had a very positive message of encouragement for the returned Jewish remnant under Zerubbabel and Joshua, but also still has a very clear and wonderfully assuring message for the Israel of future days just prior to the Millennial Kingdom. Furthermore, we, as believers, destined to be translated to heaven by Christ at the prior Resurrection and Rapture, can also derive much assurance for ourselves from the fact that Israel has a future and that the LORD will remember His promises to them. We see here that 'the LORD will remember His own' of every age and will deliver us from all oppression to enter His glorious kingdom on earth.

3. The Symbolical Crowning of Joshua the High Priest Described, verses 9-11.

As soon as the nations have been judged and the Satanic world-system has been destroyed, according to chapter 6 verses 1-8, Christ will be revealed in His Millennial Kingdom glory, as on the Mount of Transfiguration. This is now foreshadowed in verses 9-15 in the coronation of Joshua, the high priest. This symbolical act forms the climax to the revelations given in the preceding eight visions. However, the coronation of Joshua is not a vision, but a historical event, which took place in the time of Zechariah. The latter was guided in his actions at this time by a clear word from the LORD. The LORD told Zechariah to take certain men from the captivity in Babylon, who had come to Jerusalem bearing gifts which were intended to assist the returned remnant in building the temple, and to bring them to the house of Josiah the son of Zephaniah. This delegation from Babylon included men called Heldai, who is also called Helem in verse 14, Tobijah, and Jedaiah. Josiah is also called Hen in verse 14. The meanings of all these men's names are very encouraging for the discouraged remnant. Josiah means 'the LORD supports', while Hen means 'graciousness'. Heldai means 'the LORD's world', while his other name, Helem, is obscure in meaning. Tobijah means 'good is the LORD' and Jedaiah means 'the LORD knows'.

Zechariah had been well prepared to understand the deeper prophetic significance of the scene that now follows. In fact, he was to witness a prophetic fore-view of Israel's Messiah crowned as the King-Priest during the coming Millennial Kingdom. Now the LORD instructed Zechariah to take the silver and gold which the delegates from Babylon had brought as gifts with them, and from them to make an elaborate crown (literally, 'crowns', a plural of majesty), and then to set it on the head of Joshua the high priest. This was an unprecedented action to take. In the whole previous history of Israel, the priesthood and the kingship had always been separated between two different tribes and people.

4. The Messianic Significance of Joshua's Crowning Explained, verses 12-15.

The LORD now further instructed Zechariah to explain the full significance of the crowning of Joshua. He spoke as the LORD of hosts, who was acting to bless His downtrodden people Israel through it. The crowning of Joshua was a foreshadowing of the crowning of the Messiah, the divine Man, Jesus Christ. Christ will return in glory to reign as the last Adam, the second man, the King-Priest over the earth, thus regaining the dominion over God's creation which the first Adam lost through his sin of disobedience. Pilate in his ignorance directed the Jews to 'Behold the Man' (John 19.5) in humiliation, when He was crowned with thorns and bruised and scourged beyond recognition. However, the LORD had long before told them here to behold Christ in His regal capacity as the BRANCH, who is destined to renew the spiritual life and fortunes of the Davidic dynasty as the King of kings, and then to build the Millennial Temple of the LORD as the unique King-Priest. Not only will He do this, but also 'bear the glory', as a victor proudly carries the trophies of his victory in a march of triumph. He will be acknowledged as the 'KING OF KINGS, AND LORD OF LORDS' (Revelation 19. 16), the all-glorious Creator-Redeemer. Also, when He rules, the Shekinah glory cloud of the LORD's presence, which had been removed from Solomon's Temple due to Israel's persistent sins before the Exile, will return to dwell in the new temple permanently. Christ will be 'a priest upon His throne', and will be able to combine the two offices of King and Priest in perfect peace and harmony, as never before in Israel's troubled history.

In verse 14, the LORD explains to Zechariah that this elaborate crown, with which the Jews then crowned Joshua, was not subsequently to be given to the high priest, but to be laid up by the delegation from Babylon in the rebuilt second temple in Zerubbabel's day as a memorial and reminder both to them and to the prophet himself, of its typical significance for Christ in the future. Zechariah, whose name, of course, means 'whom the LORD remembers', as the prophet of Israel's ultimate hope in the promised Messiah, was given this memento to encourage him to trust in the promises of the LORD's restoring grace for Israel, which the previous eight night visions had so vividly predicted.

Finally, verse 15 states that, although it will be Christ Himself who will build the future Millennial Temple, believing Gentile nations will 'build in' it, in the sense of assisting in its construction by contributing their wealth to it; Isaiah 56. 6-7. Also, once it has been built, it will become 'a house of prayer for all nations', and many Gentile nations will come up to Jerusalem to worship there; see Isaiah 2. 2-3; 60. 1-7; Micah 4. 1-2. In verse 15, the 'Me' in the phrase, 'And ye shall know that the LORD of hosts hath sent me unto you', probably goes beyond being a reference to Zechariah as the LORD's prophet to being the words of Christ Himself, as the Angel of the LORD. Christ Himself will confirm the truth of God's Word here by building the future Millennial Temple, against all unbelieving expectations of the Jews and others since then. Participation in this scene will only be possible to those who trust and obey the voice of the LORD, Israel's God. No unbeliever will live to experience this blessing.

CHAPTER 7

The LORD Through Zechariah Answers the Question of the Delegation from Bethel concerning the Jews' Additional Fasts with a Rebuke for their Insincerity, and then Explains that the Reason for the Babylonian Exile was Israel's Disobedience to the Mosaic Law

Chapters 7-8 form the distinct middle section of Zechariah's Prophecy. These two chapters predict the same prophetic truths as are found in the night visions, but they are written in simple language, not in apocalyptic symbolism and typical events. Although they contain some rebukes, they also contain wonderful promises of encouragement concerning the restoration of Israel and the future kingdom of Christ on earth. The historical events recorded in them occurred about two years later than Zechariah's eight visions in chapters 1-6, that is, in 518 BC, Darius' fourth year, in the fourth day of the ninth month, Chislev, probably the beginning of December in our calendar. By that time the rebuilding of the second temple was progressing well, and the returned remnant had been encouraged by Darius' favourable decree issued during that year, according to Ezra chapter 6 verses 1-14. The future now looked more promising for the Jews. Therefore, the question arose in their minds as to whether, or not, it was necessary for them any longer to observe the additional fasts which had been started to commemorate the anniversaries of their calamities, namely, the fall of Jerusalem and the burning of Solomon's Temple on the tenth day of the fifth month (2 Kings 25.8-9), and also the murder of Gedaliah, the governor appointed by the Babylonians to rule the defeated Jews after the fall of the city, in the seventh month; see 2 Kings 25.25 and Jeremiah 41. Neither of these additional fast days, unlike the annual Day of Atonement of Leviticus chapters 16 and 23, had originally been instituted or commanded by the LORD, and the returning Jews realised this fact. Hence their concern, but they may not have prepared for the LORD's replies to them.

1. The Question about the Jews' Additional Fasts Observed since the Fall of Jerusalem Answered, verses 1-7.

Verse 2 in the AV reads as follows: 'When they had sent unto the house of God Sherezer and Regem-melech, and their men, to pray before the LORD...', but M.F. Unger points out that the correct translation of the verse should read thus: 'Now the town of Bethel had sent Sharezer and Regem-melech and their men to seek the favour of the LORD'. 'Bethel' is the name of the place in Israel, not a reference to the temple, and it should be the subject of the sentence. Sharezer and Regem-melech are given their Babylonian names to show that they were Jewish exiles who had returned from Babylon. These men were evidently important leaders in their city, because they had a retinue sent to accompany them. They had come to appease the LORD. In verse 3, therefore, speaking as one man for the whole city of Bethel, they asked the priests and prophets of the LORD in the temple while it was in the process of being rebuilt, 'Should I weep in the fifth month, and fast, as I have done these so many years?' The LORD replied very promptly to their enquiry, and asked them whether they had really been fasting and mourning in the fifth and seventh months for the past seventy years in order to glorify and please Him, or whether it was really an insincere act of self-pity for the consequences of their sins which had made their exile inevitable. The full answer to the delegates' enquiry was not in fact given by the LORD until chapter 8 verses 18-19. Here, in chapter 7, He exposed their hypocrisy and selfishness in observing these additional fasts, which He had never required of them.

This further word of the LORD through Zechariah was to remind them that they should have listened to, and obeyed, the messages of the pre-exilic prophets, who had warned Israel and Judah of the danger of disobedience to the LORD's word in days when the country was enjoying relative prosperity and all its cities were fully populated. These messages, which have largely been preserved in our Bibles, gave sufficient instruction to the then-present generation of Jews to enable them to understand how to please the LORD and to continue to live in peace and prosperity in their own land. The LORD does not always answer our questions in the way we hope and expect, because He reads the inner motives of our hearts, and first answers the underlying sinful problems which our often misguided questions reveal about us. The Lord Jesus often so dealt with men and women who approached Him with questions during His public ministry, as the four Gospels record.

2. The Real Cause of the Babylonian Exile Explained, verses 8-14.

In His second message to the delegation from Bethel in verses 8-14, the LORD through Zechariah clearly spelt out the cause of the recent Babylonian Exile as plain disobedience to His word through all the previous prophets. He had clearly said to all the generations of Israel and Judah that He expected social justice from them, the respect of the rights of the poor and widows, and a demonstration of mercy and compassion towards their fellowmen and women. Sadly, He said that those generations had refused to listen to His word, and had deliberately hardened their hearts like flint against obeying the words of the Law, which the previous prophets had continually proclaimed to them. Therefore, and for no other reason, great wrath had fallen on them from the LORD of hosts, who, we should remember, can use His almighty power to judge, as well as to bless, His people Israel. The result was that, just as the LORD had cried out to them to listen to Him, and they had refused, so later, before the fall of Jerusalem, when the people of God had cried out to Him for help in their distress, He had refused to listen to them and to help them. God is not mocked: what we sow, we reap; it is an inevitable moral law of God's governmental ways with mankind. Let us be warned to obey the word of God as soon as we hear and understand it! This was why the LORD scattered Israel and Judah with judgements like a whirlwind among all the Gentile nations whom they did not know. Also, this was why their Promised Land became desolate after they had been deported from it; for the Gentile nations had laid their previously 'pleasant land' (literally, 'land of desire, or delight') completely waste. Furthermore, it fully explains why the land of Israel, which was more than once in the Old Testament described as the pleasant, or glorious, land (see Psalm 106. 24; Jeremiah 3.19; Daniel 11. 16, 41), and which the LORD originally said to His earthly people was 'flowing with milk and honey', became for so many long centuries a barren wilderness, until very recent times, when the LORD has begun to regather them back into it, although at first in unbelief, in preparation for the end-time events and their full restoration in the Millennial Kingdom.

CHAPTER 8

The LORD Through Zechariah Promises Israel Complete Restoration During the Millennial Kingdom and Gives them the Answer to their Question about the Additional Fasts

If chapter 7 has given the Jewish delegation the negative aspect of the LORD's answer to their question about the observance of their additional fasts, chapter 8 gives them the positive and encouraging reply to it. Chapter 7 had been a call to repentance and a reminder that Israel's past calamities, and the Babylonian Exile in particular, had been the direct consequence of their disobedience to God's word. In chapter 8, Zechariah was inspired to foretell that Israel's fasts would all one day change into feasts as a result of the LORD's sovereign grace and love alone, but he emphasised that obedience to God's word was still the indispensable prerequisite for the blessings that are promised here. So the question about the fasts was answered in a far better way than the enquirers in chapter 7 could ever have anticipated; see Ephesians 3. 20.

1. Israel's Then-Present Partial Restoration is the Assurance of Their Eventual Full Restoration, verses 1-8.

In these verses, we are reminded that prophetic truth concerning the future always has an intended effect on our present moral and spiritual condition. Here the LORD through Zechariah assures Israel that He will one day fully restore them to their land again in peace and prosperity. This will be fulfilled in the Millennial Kingdom. In verse 2, He declares that He is acting in great jealousy for His people, and with great zeal for their welfare. Just as His jealousy has previously been the reason why He judged them for their sins against His holiness, so now His jealousy for them as His chosen earthly people motivated Him to restore them to greater peace and happiness than they had ever known before in their history. In verse 3, He promises to return to Zion and dwell again in the midst of Jerusalem. Ezekiel tells us that this will happen after Israel are restored spiritually and regathered to their land again, as the LORD's Shekinah glory cloud returns to dwell in the Millennial Temple, and Jerusalem is called JEHOVAH Shammah, 'The LORD is there'; see Ezekiel 43. 1-5; 48. 35. Jerusalem during the coming kingdom of Christ will be known as the city of truth and holiness, by contrast with its condition before that time. Verses 4-5 predict scenes in the city of complete peace and security, as old men and women are seen living safely and happily in it, and boys and girls play in its streets quite undisturbed and unafraid. This wonderful prediction will seem extraordinary to the restored remnant of Israel, who will experience these blessings in those coming days of the Millennial Kingdom, but it is nothing surprising to the LORD of hosts, who has almighty ability to bring it to pass in His own time for His oppressed people. Therefore, let the Jews of Zerubbabel's day be encouraged to continue in their work of reconstruction, since the LORD of hosts was in control of the whole situation despite its difficulties.

The LORD further predicts that He will save His scattered people Israel from both the east country and the west country, where they have been dispersed for their sins against Him, and regather them back to dwell again in Jerusalem. Then He will own them once more as His people, and they will willingly acknowledge Him to be their God, and live in accordance with His truth and righteousness. In our own day this process of the regathering of Israel to their Promised Land has begun, since the latter half of the nineteenth century, but, as Ezekiel's prophecy has predicted, they are as yet in unbelief. However, Israel will be revived spiritually as well as nationally, and will enter the kingdom as a saved nation, as Zechariah chapters 12-14 indicate; see also Ezekiel 36-37.

2. The LORD Encourages the Jewish Remnant in the Hardships of the Then-Present Partial Restoration, verses 9-17.

Although the wonderful revelations given to Zechariah will only be finally fulfilled in the coming Millennial Kingdom, Zechariah now makes a contemporary application of them to the returned remnant of Jews from Babylon who are rebuilding the temple. He encouraged them to continue the work of rebuilding, despite the difficulties which they had already encountered for over fifteen years. The builders had been discouraged, because they had not received wages for doing the work, and also because there were strained social relationships among the builders, in addition to opposition from their Gentile enemies around them. In fact, the LORD had allowed this situation to develop, because they had not put Him first in their lives, but, in verses 11-15, the LORD assures His people that He had ceased His controversy with them, and would henceforth bless and assist them in their work. In verse 12, He promises them prosperity in their farming. Then, in verse 13, He promises that His people would cease to be a curse among the surrounding Gentile nations, and be a blessing instead. This transformation from their being a curse to being a blessing will ultimately occur as a result of their acceptance of their Messiah. In view of their glorious future, Zechariah urged the returned remnant not to fear their enemies and difficulties, but to redouble their efforts to build the temple, for the LORD had now decided to do them good, not harm. He was no longer punishing them for their fathers' sins, which had provoked His wrath and had led to the Exiles. Only, they needed to practise social justice and truth, and live in peace with one another. They should not meditate to do evil to one another, nor practise falsehood. The LORD hates such evils, and will withhold His blessing again, if these things are found among them.

3. The LORD Promises Israel's Full Restoration to Joy, Peace, and Favour with both God and Men, verses 18-23.

The LORD had shown His people the insincerity of their additional fasts, about which they had consulted Him. He had also pointed out to them the sins which had caused their past calamities. Now therefore, as a result of their repentance, He was able to reveal to them the divine blessing which would be theirs, in part at that time, but in full in the future Millennial Kingdom. Also, He was now prepared to answer their enquiry concerning the fasts, out of which this whole prophecy had arisen. The LORD's answer was that all these various fasts would cease to be occasions of mourning, and become feasts, occasions of joy and blessing. Isaiah had also foreseen this transformation of fasts to feasts; see Isaiah 65. 19. The LORD here adds two additional fasts which have not been previously mentioned, namely, one on the tenth day of the tenth month, which marked the beginning of the siege of Jerusalem by Nebuchadnezzar, and another on the ninth day of the fourth month, which marked the day when Nebuchadnezzar breached the wall of the city and captured it; see 2 Kings 25.1-3. Only, if they wanted these fasts to become feasts, they must continue to love and practise truth and peace both with Him and with one another.

Verses 20-23 contain some remarkable millennial predictions concerning Israel in the Millennial Kingdom. Then all nations on earth will come spontaneously to pray to the LORD in Jerusalem, and everyone will recognise that the LORD is with the Jews and wish to join them in their worship; see Chapter 14. 16-19; Isaiah 2. 3. Such will be the popularity of the LORD's chosen people in that glorious future day, by contrast with their downtrodden condition in both Zerubbabel's time and our own day. What a complete reversal of fortunes the LORD can accomplish when conditions in His people are right!

CHAPTER 9

The Beginning of Zechariah's First Prophetic Oracle Concerning the First and Second Comings of Christ

The two prophetic 'burdens', 'oracles', or prophetic messages in chapters 9-14 of Zechariah's Prophecy form the second major half of the book. They are identical in scope and prophetic truth with those of the first half of the book, although they are presented in a somewhat different form from the first half with its eight apocalyptic night visions. Unlike the visions of chapters 1-6 and the messages of chapters 7-8, they are undated. This has led some commentators to suggest that they were not written by Zechariah, but by a later prophet. However, the correspondences between the two halves of the book in subject matter are so strong that it is better to suppose that chapters 9-14 were written by Zechariah much later in his life, perhaps after the kingdom of Greece had begun to make its mark in the history of the Near East in the early fifth century BC. Neither the Septuagint nor the traditions of the Jews divide the book at this point, which consideration supports the book's unity of authorship. In fact, these last six chapters envisage Israel under four different rules. Whereas chapters 1-8 had envisaged Israel under Medo-Persian rule, chapters 9-10 envisage Israel under the rule of the Grecian kings, chapter 11 probably envisages them under Roman rule, and chapters 12-14 refer entirely to times yet future to us today, when Israel will be under the rule of the Antichrist, followed by the direct rule of Christ in the Millennial Kingdom. The historical and prophetic scope of the book is thus very wide and far-reaching. Simple believers in the almighty power of God to predict the future, which He also controls, find no difficulty in accepting it all as literally as is reasonably possible. Many of these predictions have clearly already been fulfilled, while the remainder will be fulfilled in a time probably not too far distant from our own day.

These two prophetic messages, therefore, primarily concern the two comings of Christ: first, His past coming in grace and humility to die; secondly, His future coming in glory and power to judge and to reign. The first prophetic message in chapters 9-11 predicts both His first coming in grace and His second coming in glory, whereas the second message in chapters 12-14 predicts only His second coming after the Great Tribulation. Chapter 11 predicts the rejection of Christ at His first coming, and its consequences for the Jewish nation then. All these chapters are very rich in their presentation of Christ in the varied aspects of His character, life, and work. The reader should notice how accurate were Zechariah's predictions of Christ, and how literally his prophecies were fulfilled at Christ's first coming. These chapters not only encourage us today to believe all God's promises for the future, but would have encouraged their original readers in the later days of the return of the Jews from Babylon to continue steadfastly in their worship and service for the LORD. Israel certainly has a future in God's purposes which no-one can frustrate, since the LORD has not rejected them forever. He will yet choose them, save them, and bring them into eternal blessing.

Chapter 9 can best be divided into three parts. Verses 1-8 appear to predict the campaigns and conquests of Alexander the Great in Syria and Palestine after his victory over the Persians at the Battle of Issus in 333 BC. Verses 9-11 predict the first coming of Christ and His entry into Jerusalem in about AD 33, then look forward to His millennial reign. Verses 12-17 concern mainly the conflicts of the Maccabaean Jews with the Grecian rulers of Palestine in the second century BC, but also look beyond that time to the final restoration of Israel. As we proceed in the commentary, we shall note that Zechariah omits all reference to the present Church Age between the first and second comings of Christ, which was then a mystery hidden in God from all Ages previous to the present one; see Ephesians 3. 3-10; Colossians 1. 25-27. This so-called 'prophetic gap' is found in many parts of Old Testament prophetic Scripture.

1. The LORD's Judgement on Israel's Neighbouring Nations through the Campaigns of Alexander the Great, but His Miraculous Protection of Israel from Invasion by Alexander, verses 1-8.

Alexander the Great was probably the immediate human

cause of the destruction described in these verses, since the order of the cities named here corresponds with Alexander's known line of march through Syria and Palestine after his defeat of the Persian army at Issus in 333 BC. However, he is not mentioned here, because the LORD was the ultimate divine cause of the judgements on these enemies of Israel. Alexander was simply an instrument in His sovereign hand. Hadrach was probably Hatarika, an Aramaean country near Damascus and Hamath mentioned in Assyrian inscriptions. Damascus was the capital of Syria; the LORD's wrath was abiding on that city. The end of verse 1 means that, while everyone's eyes, including those of Israel, would be on Alexander's progress through the lands as he was conquering them, they would really be looking at the LORD's acts of judgement through him. Hamath was in Syria, north of Damascus. The Phoenician cities of Tyre and Sidon would not be immune from Alexander's attack either, although they were renowned for their human wisdom. Verses 3-4 predict the fall of Tyre to Alexander in 332 BC after a short five-month siege. Although Tyre was an island stronghold built on a rock, and had acquired a vast fortune of silver and gold through maritime trading, the sovereign Lord GOD of Israel would allow Alexander to destroy it by fire. Both the Assyrians and the Babylonians had previously failed to conquer Tyre decisively after long sieges.

Next in the line of Alexander's advancing armies were the four Philistine cities of Ashkelon, Gaza, Ekron, and Ashdod. They also would fall to Alexander, and he would kill the king of Ekron. Gath, the fifth Philistine city, is not mentioned here, probably because at that time it had become part of Judah. A mixed race would come to live in Ashdod after its conquest, and the Philistines' national pride would be humbled. The survivors of the Philistines would be cleansed from their polluted idolatry, in preparation for their being incorporated into the kingdom of Judah, as Araunah the Jebusite and some other foreigners had been in past centuries; see 2 Samuel 24. 15-25; 1 Chronicles 21. 18-29.

Verse 8 predicts that the LORD would divinely protect His temple in Jerusalem from attack by Alexander as he passed by Israel in the course of his campaigns. Josephus records that the Jewish high priest, Jaddua, having received a dream from the

LORD, met Alexander near Jerusalem with a delegation of peace, and won his favour, so that he decided to leave the Jewish kingdom alone. Perhaps Jaddua may have told Alexander concerning the prophecies in the Scriptures which mention him in a fairly complimentary light. However, the end of verse 8 goes beyond the time of Jerusalem's deliverance in the time of Alexander, and assures Israel that there will come a time when 'no oppressor shall pass through them any more'. This anticipates the Millennial Kingdom, after Christ has delivered them for the last time from all their surrounding enemies; see chapter 14. 3. The LORD, who has always watched over His chosen people will bring this to pass.

2. The LORD Predicts the First Coming of Israel's Messianic King in Lowliness and Justice, by Contrast with Alexander the Great, and then Christ's Second Coming to Rule in Peace and Glory, verses 9-11.

Now, however, against the prophetic background of Alexander's victorious campaigns in Palestine, we are introduced to the LORD's true and perfect monarch, who contrasts with the proud, warlike, and ambitious Alexander, and will become the LORD's final instrument to accomplish all His purposes on earth in a kingdom of peace and righteousness. Israel is exhorted to rejoice greatly at the coming of this truly-qualified King. Not only is He righteous and humble, but He comes bringing salvation with Him. The end of verse 9 was fulfilled on Palm Sunday, when, as Matthew's Gospel records in chapter 21 verses 4-7, Christ made His triumphal entry into Jerusalem riding on an ass and a colt, the foal of an ass, a double picture of His peaceful intentions then. In every way, Christ was a complete contrast to Alexander the Great, the human conqueror, who was noted for his violent injustice at times and sought world conquest for his own glory. Alexander, the ruthless warrior and international bully, rode a prancing black steed aptly named Bucephalus, which means 'bull-headed', the most famous horse in antiquity; Christ, God's future benevolent King of kings, rode a lowly and borrowed ass, the symbol of humility and peace.

Between verses 9 and 10 lies the prophetic gap, which we have already explained. Verse 10 looks beyond the Church Age to the beginning of Christ's Millennial Kingdom. Then the LORD in the Person of His Son, the Prince of Peace, will cause all wars to cease, destroy all armaments, and introduce world-wide peace. Christ will speak words of peace to the Gentile nations and reign over every part of the earth, from the River Euphrates to the very furthest boundaries of the world. The latter half of verse 10 is a quotation from Psalm 72 verse 8, a millennial Psalm written by Solomon, the typical king of peace. In verse 11 the LORD gives an additional assurance to the nation of Israel that, because of the covenant which He has ratified with them by the blood of a vicarious sacrifice, He has sent those of them who were prisoners in captivity out of the waterless dungeon in which they had been held, like Joseph before he was sold into Egypt by his brothers. Many commentators see 'the covenant' referred to as the Mosaic covenant. This was, of course, a conditional one. For this reason the present writer prefers to think that it refers to the several unconditional covenants which the LORD had made with His people, from the Abrahamic and the Palestinian Covenants to the Davidic Covenant. These alone would guarantee the LORD's certain action in deliverance, because they depended for their fulfilment upon Himself alone. Thus the LORD encouraged His downtrodden people after Zerubbabel's day to trust Him for continued deliverance and help in all their trials of faith. They now had Him as their sure Hope after all their difficulties in exile.

3. The Prediction of the Maccabaean Jews' Victory over the Greek Seleucid kings, which Foreshadows their Final Salvation by the LORD at the Beginning of the Millennial Kingdom, verses 12-17.

In verse 12, the LORD reminds His people, whom He had recently delivered from exile, to turn to Him as their stronghold. If they do this, then He promises to restore them to a double portion of His blessing as His firstborn nation in the world. He would not always chastise them for their past disobedience. Verses 13-15 predict the struggles and victories of the faithful Jews in the second century BC against the ruling Greek Seleucid kings, who were idolatrous and attempted to compel the Jews to adopt their own idolatrous ways. This Maccabaean struggle was only going to be a foreshadowing of Israel's final, still future, conflict with the nations before her kingdom blessing was received. The reference to the sons of Greece in verse 13 is a reference to the

Jews' war with the Seleucid kings, in which they were victorious for a considerable time. In verses 14-15, the LORD promises to protect them and to fight for them. This applied in the time of the Maccabees and will apply in the future. The victorious Jews will become filled and bespattered with the blood of their defeated enemies. Verse 16 promises that the LORD will save them in that day, that is, in the future Day of the LORD, when Christ comes the second time to reign and to judge. He will act as their Good Shepherd caring for them, His chosen flock. He will regard and treat them like the jewels of a crown, and lift them up like a banner of victory over His Promised Land. This is a beautiful picture of restored and regathered Israel in their land again. Finally, verse 17 contains an expression of appreciation of the LORD, probably by the prophet Zechariah himself. He extols both the great goodness of the LORD and His great beauty. In the coming Millennial Kingdom, the young men will thrive on the abundance of the grain crops, and the young women will thrive on the new wine of joy that they can enjoy. Such will be Israel's blessing and privilege then, due entirely to the LORD's sovereign covenant grace! When once Israel have acknowledged their Messiah's grace, goodness, and beauty, and have given Him His rightful place in their lives, then material prosperity and abundance will soon follow. Chapter 10 verse 1 really concludes this present chapter with an assurance of the blessing upon nature that Christ will bring in His kingdom, but we shall consider it fully with the next chapter.

CHAPTER 10

The LORD Promises to Strengthen both Judah and Ephraim to Overcome their Enemies, and to Redeem, Regather, and Restore His Scattered People from their Worldwide Dispersion

Chapter 10 continues the themes of Israel's restoration and ultimate victory in the Millennial Kingdom which the latter part of chapter 9 had begun.

1. Christ will Destroy the False Shepherds of Israel at His Second Coming, verses 1-5.

The LORD requests His people to ask Him to send the latter rain, which falls in late April and early May, so that the abundance of grain and wine spoken of at the end of chapter 9 may be granted to them. They should not ask for it by any magical and forbidden occult means, but from its true source, the LORD Himself. The LORD says this, because Israel has had sad experience in the past of trying to gain material prosperity by idolatrous means, such as the worship of the Baals and the use of teraphim. Such idolatry had been the cause of their wandering away from Him spiritually and falling into trouble. Israel had often been following either no shepherds or the wrong kind of shepherds to guide and lead them. The LORD's anger was aroused against the shepherds of Israel and Judah, their kings who had led them astray. These kings are also described as he-goats, that is, aggressive and oppressive in their rule, because they were responsible for leading them wrongly. They would be punished for this. The LORD now said that He was going to visit His people Judah as their Good Shepherd to bless them, and make them like His majestic royal horse in His battle against their enemies.

Then verse 4 describes the coming Messiah in four unique ways as He will deliver and protect His people in a day yet future to us; see chapter 14. Christ would come out of Judah, and be like a cornerstone to His people, the firm foundation on Whom they could build their lives. He would also be like a nail, or tent-peg, stable and reliable for His people to trust themselves to. Further, He would be like a battle bow to fight their enemies, as He will at Armageddon as their Divine Warrior. Finally, He would come out of Judah as the divinely ordained Ruler in the Millennial Kingdom; see Genesis 49. 10; Micah 5. 2. However, we should here take some account of the other possible way of understanding this fourth phrase; for M.F. Unger and C.L. Feinberg take it in a bad sense relating to Israel's oppressors, not in a good sense relating to Christ. They understand the phrase to mean that through Christ's intervention at His second coming all Israel's oppressors will be made to depart from them. Both interpretations are possible, although in the context of the previous descriptions of Christ, the first, the good, sense is perhaps to be preferred.

Whatever the correct interpretation of the end of verse 4 may be, verse 5 continues by revealing that it will not only be Christ who will fight their enemies; the people of Judah themselves will be empowered to fight them like mighty men, or heroes. They will tread down their enemies like mud in the streets in the battle of that day, the day of Armageddon. Because the LORD will be with them, the enemies on their horses, in which kind of warfare the nations of the Near East were normally superior to the armies of Israel, will be put to shame by the men of Judah's military prowess. Christ's appearance at His second coming will consummate Israel's deliverance. Thus all Israel's former false shepherds, that is, oppressing leaders, will be destroyed.

2. Christ will Regather all Israel to their Promised Land at His Second Coming, verses 6-12.

Now the LORD promises to strengthen both the house of Judah and the house of Joseph, which is a reference to the northern tribes. This is made clear in verse 7, where Ephraim is mentioned, so that all Israel is included in this blessing. He says that He will bring them back from their dispersion and cause them to dwell in their Promised Land again. The converted and restored Jewish remnant, which will constitute the nation in the coming kingdom, will enjoy the LORD's favour again as if they had never been cast off for a time. The LORD is their God and He will listen to their cries for help and salvation. The tribes of Ephraim, the northern part of the divided kingdom, will be like a mighty man, or hero, in war, and rejoice in the LORD their God from the heart.

In verses 8-11, the LORD promises to regather and restore all Israel from the lands to which He previously scattered them, and to bring them into their own land again in such numbers that no more room will be found for them there. This will occur after He has first redeemed them, that is, after their national regeneration promised in the new covenant through the prophets Jeremiah and Ezekiel; see Jeremiah 31. 31-34; Ezekiel 36-37. Zechariah himself predicts their national contrition, conversion, and cleansing in chapters 12-13. The nation will become as large as it once was before their dispersion. In their various locations around the world at the beginning of the Millennial Kingdom, the surviving and believing Israelites will remember the LORD and return to Him again. Then He will whistle or pipe to them, like a shepherd calling His flock, and He will bring them all out of all their former enemies' countries, including both Egypt and Assyria in the north and the south, into their own land, which is here associated with Gilead and Lebanon. It will be like a second Exodus out of Egypt through the Red Sea; all obstacles will be removed to facilitate their return. At last, the pride, power, and independent sovereignty of their bitterest enemies will be humbled and removed. In fact, Isaiah chapter 19 predicts that Egypt and Assyria will in that day join Israel in worshipping the LORD and will be equally blessed. Such will be the transformation in the world situation that the LORD will achieve then!

Finally, in verse 12, the LORD again promises to strengthen His people in their relationship with Himself. Note that the way in which this verse is phrased implies the tri-unity of God, since the 'I' is a divine Person, as well as the LORD. The saved Israelite remnant will have full freedom to live in a way that glorifies the Name of the LORD, and become His missionaries to the whole world, as they were originally intended to be. Walking to and fro in His Name implies that they will witness with great zeal and power, as the apostle Paul did to the Gentiles at the start of the Church Age, to all the millennial nations.

We are today living in momentous days, as we are seeing before our eyes the beginnings of Israel's regathering as an independent sovereign nation in their own Promised Land. In fact, the process has been going on now for well over a hundred years, since the latter half of the nineteenth century, and especially since the establishment of the State of Israel in 1948. We should recognise, however, that this is not the final fulfilment of these Old Testament prophecies and promises, but only the necessary preparation for their fulfilment. God cannot fully bless His ancient chosen earthly people before they are converted to Christ, their True Shepherd and Messiah, when He appears in glory at His second coming to earth to judge and reign. Much is predicted to happen before that moment, including the Resurrection and Rapture of the Church saints, followed by the terrible time of Tribulation spoken about in so many Scriptures in both Testaments. The dreadful rule of the Antichrist must first be allowed to take its course, before the true Christ returns to assert His authority and rectify all the damage which that ruler will cause. Of this we may still be certain, however, that the Pre-millennial understanding of Scripture is gradually being confirmed as true, and that our own prior redemption and rapture to heaven is drawing very near. Maranatha! The Lord is coming! Amen!

CHAPTER 11

The LORD Explains that the Impending Devastation of the Land of Israel would be due to Israel's Rejection of their Good Shepherd and their Acceptance of the False Shepherd

This most sad chapter, which is very significantly juxtaposed with a chapter concerning Israel's future hope, explains the reason why there has been such a long delay in Israel's realising the blessings promised in chapter 10. It may be divided into three main sections: first, verses 1-3 contain a lamentation over the coming devastation of the land of Israel; secondly, verses 4-14 predict the rejection of the Good Shepherd; thirdly, verses 15-17 predict the evil character and severe judgement of the False Shepherd whom Israel will accept.

1. Zechariah's Lamentation over the Coming Devastation of the Land of Israel by the Romans, verses 1-3.

The vivid description of the devastation of the Promised Land in verses 1-3, if it is considered in isolation from its context, could be related to more than one period in Israel's troubled history. However, the immediate context of the rejection of Israel's Good Shepherd in the main section of the chapter which follows, strongly suggests that the particular invasion of the land which is in mind here is that of the Romans in the years surrounding the fall of Jerusalem in AD 70. This was a judgement on the Jews for their rejection and crucifixion of Christ. The description should probably be understood quite literally, not in any symbolical way. References to the destruction of the cedars of Lebanon, the oaks of Bashan, and the lush thickets of the Jordan Valley suggest the devastation of the entire land of Israel from north to south and from east to west. All three areas were then heavily forested, but have since then, and until very recent times, been a barren wilderness. Shepherds would wail, because they had lost the pastures which their flocks needed, and even the young lions would roar in anguish, because the thick jungles in which they made their lairs around the Jordan had been ruined. The LORD through Zechariah presents to us the results of the rejection of Christ in the form of a poetical lamentation, before He tells him to enact in some detail the real cause of the judgement on the land of Israel.

2. The LORD tells Zechariah to Enact a Prophetic Parable concerning Israel's Culpable Rejection of their Good Shepherd, verses 4-14.

In this quite long and difficult centre section of the chapter Zechariah declares that the LORD his God has instructed him to enact a prophetic parable before his hearers and readers that explains the circumstances in which his people Israel would reject their Good Shepherd. Although not every phrase in this passage can easily be understood with certainty, its main subject is quite clear in the light of its fulfilment at Christ's first coming in grace and humility.

In verse 4, God told Zechariah to tend the flock which was destined for slaughter. The flock was the LORD's people Israel, and the verse is saying that, because of what occurs in the subsequent passage, Israel is destined to be slaughtered by the Romans in the siege of Jerusalem in AD 70. Verses 5-6 then describe the predicted punishment of the Jews at that time. Their own leaders would fail in their duty to pity and protect them. This is true, whether 'they that sell them' are the Jewish leaders or the foreign oppressors. More sadly still, the LORD Himself would no longer have pity on them, but allow them to become the victims of internal civil strife and the Roman 'king', or Caesar. They would one day remember that they had foolishly cried out to Pilate at the trial of Christ, 'We have no king but Caesar'. Therefore, the LORD would leave them to their Caesar's 'tender mercies'; He would not deliver them from the Roman armies.

In verse 7, Zechariah did as the LORD had instructed him, and portrayed the work of a shepherd tending the flock of Israel destined for slaughter for the sake of those who are described as 'the poor of the flock'. They are probably the faithful Jewish remnant of believers at the first coming of Christ, introduced to us in the Gospel records, especially in Luke's opening chapters. As any good shepherd would, Zechariah took for his work of shepherding two staffs to guide and to protect the flock. One he called Beauty, the other he called Bands. They represented the LORD's gracious favour and blessings on His people, and the internal union of Israel and Judah as one nation.

Verses 8-9 are a little more obscure to us today, but probably relate to the leaders of Israel's rejection of Christ at his first coming. Zechariah does not explain who the 'three shepherds' are whom he was to cut off in one month, but they are probably to be understood to be the three classes of leaders who were anointed to administer Israel for God, namely, prophets, priests, and kings. Alternatively, they may refer to the Pharisees, Sadducees, and Herodians. Zechariah here represents Christ when he says that His soul loathed them, while they detested Him. The Four Gospel records contain abundant evidence of the truth of these statements. Christ could not tolerate the hypocrisy of the Jewish leaders of His day, nor did they want Him, but sought by every means to destroy Him. The climactic events leading up to Christ's crucifixion took place in one momentous month. Therefore, Zechariah, again representing Christ, declares that He is giving up His role as His people's Shepherd, and is leaving the flock, the Jewish people, to suffer their inevitable fate at the hands of their enemies. There was even some cannibalism during the siege of Jerusalem in AD 70, and certainly much in-fighting among the Jews.

In verses 10-11, Christ through Zechariah explains the result of His decisive rejection by His own nation. It would be nothing less than the setting aside of Israel for a time as the LORD's covenant people, as Romans chapter 11 asserts.

Accordingly, Zechariah took hold of his staff called Beauty and chopped it to pieces. This signified that the LORD was breaking His covenant with all the Gentile nations, which had restrained them from attacking and conquering Israel. Consequently, the Romans would be allowed to invade His land successfully and disperse His earthly people to all the countries of the world. However, the end of verse 11 reveals that there were a few faithful believing Jews, who are again called 'the poor of the flock', who were watching and waiting upon their God. They would recognise that all these disastrous events for their nation were in fulfilment of the word of the LORD through His faithful prophets, such as Zechariah.

Verses 12-13 are the saddest verses in this passage. Here Christ, represented by Zechariah as Israel's Good Shepherd, asks His people, if they were in agreement, to name His value, or wages, for all His work of shepherding them down the years. Tragically, the Jews named His price as a mere thirty pieces of silver, the price paid to the master of a slave who had been gored by an ox, and was therefore disabled; see Exodus 21.32. Christ's contemporaries grossly underestimated His real worth. The thirty pieces of silver, for which Judas Iscariot betrayed Christ according to the Gospel records, was a gross insult both to Him and to the LORD who had sent Him. Most men still undervalue Christ's worth today. The LORD's reaction in indignation was to tell Zechariah to fling the thirty pieces of silver into the house of the potter, who was considered to be one of the lowest workers in Jewish society. The sad irony in the LORD's voice is very poignant, as He says that it was 'a goodly price that I was prized at of them'. Zechariah did as the LORD had instructed him, and flung the silver to the potter in the house of the LORD. Here the fulfilment by Judas Iscariot, recorded in Matthew chapter 27 verses 3-10, explains the precise interpretation of this sentence in Zechariah. The money was flung down in the temple and immediately taken up by the priests to purchase the field of a potter for a burying-ground for the poor. Matthew ascribes this quotation from Zechariah to Jeremiah, not Zechariah. According to M.F. Unger, the best explanation of this unexpected reference is probably that Matthew was citing this passage from a roll of the prophets by the name of the first book, in which, according to the Talmudic tradition, the prophetic writings were placed in the Jewish canon. This was apparently Jeremiah. Compare Luke chapter 24 verse 44 for a similar practice, where the book of Psalms gives its name to the entire third section of the Hebrew canon.

Verse 14 predicts the final abandonment of the Jewish nation for the time being. Zechariah cut into pieces his other staff, Bands, which symbolised the unity of Israel. Internal discord was one of the factors which led to the destruction of Jerusalem in AD 70, and to the subsequent dispersion of the Jews worldwide.

3. The LORD further Instructs Zechariah to enact a Prophetic Parable concerning Israel's Acceptance of the False Shepherd and his Judgement, verses 15-17.

Having enacted the part of the Good Shepherd in His rejection, Zechariah is now instructed to take up the implements of a foolish shepherd, that is, to enact, by contrast, a further prophetic parable concerning Israel's still future acceptance of another professed shepherd, the Antichrist of the Tribulation period, to declare the evil character of that False Shepherd, and his severe judgement by God. Thus Israel will one day compound their tragic mistake in rejecting the true Christ by accepting the False Christ. The rule of the Antichrist will actually be the LORD's judgement on the nation for their rejection of His Son incarnate; for He says in verse 16 that He will raise the Antichrist up to misrule His people. The Antichrist will fail to fulfil any of the duties of a good and responsible shepherd of the LORD's people. He will have no concern for the flock and its needs, but will be interested only in exploiting the people for his own selfish gratification, regardless of the suffering which he is causing them. He will be foolish, worthless, evil, and idolatrous, as other Scriptures indicate, since he will demand universal worship as if he were God. Therefore, verse 17 pronounces judgement upon him for his negligence of his charges. Both his strength, 'his arm', and his intelligence, 'his right eye', will, as it were, be pierced by the LORD's sword. His strength will be completely dried up, and his right eye be utterly blinded. In fact, his end is destruction in the Lake of Fire; Revelation 19. 20.

**Introduction to Zechariah's Grand Finale
in His Second Oracle, Chapters 12-14**

Chapter 11 described events which are completely hopeless and tragic. It began with the sight of Israel's Promised Land in utter devastation, then continued with their culpable rejection and gross underestimation of their True and Good Shepherd's worth, with its consequences in the nation's worldwide dispersion, and ended with their suffering, by the LORD's sovereign permissive will, under the despotic rule of the Evil and False Shepherd, the Antichrist, whom they will accept, until the LORD decisively judges him in outer darkness and the torments of the Lake of Fire. The question must therefore be asked, 'After all their calamitous history, how can Israel ever realise their hope of restoration, which the LORD has clearly promised them in the earlier chapters of this prophecy?' Are Amillennialists and Replacement Theologians right when they assert that, as a result of their rejection of Christ at His first coming, Israel has forfeited all their privileges and promises as God's chosen earthly people to the New Testament Church since Pentecost? Is the Church now the 'New and True Israel'? Has the present Church inherited all Israel's Old Testament promises in only a spiritualised way? Will there now never be a literal Millennial Kingdom of Christ on earth?

Thankfully, Zechariah's second burden, or oracle, in chapters 12-14, decisively proves that the LORD has neither finally rejected His earthly people Israel for their many sins, nor allowed their total destruction by their enemies, but will ultimately deliver them, regenerate them, and cleanse them at Christ's glorious second coming to judge and reign over a literal thousand-year kingdom on earth in holiness and peace. No, the LORD has not fully given them up, but will yet 'remember His Own', return to them the second time, and be accepted by them then. Yes, Israel's hope of full restoration is certain on the basis of their very same sinful act of rejecting and crucifying their Messiah; for there on the Cross the LORD was punishing Christ, His Son, on behalf of all His people's sins as a vicarious sacrifice. God in Christ paid the penalty for them, as Isaiah chapter 53 several times explains. How this magnifies His sovereign mercy, love, grace, wisdom, and power! Truly, His ways are past finding out, as Paul's doxology in Romans chapter 11 declares! In Romans chapters 9-11, Paul fully explains what God has been doing with His earthly people Israel during the present Church Age, and then predicts their national conversion at Christ's second coming. Yes, as Zechariah's second oracle here predicts also, Israel has a future, initially very traumatic, but ultimately very glorious and blessed in every way. These three chapters to which we now turn are the death-knell of Amillennialism and Replacement Theology, which are so prevalent in many local churches today. Here is what a literal reading of them states. Let us believe them in simple faith, however unlikely we think it is that they can ever be fulfilled.

CHAPTER 12

Israel's Deliverance in the Future Siege of Jerusalem and their National Repentance and Conversion at Christ's Glorious Second Coming

The events which are predicted in chapters 12-14 almost all concern the future time period of the Day of the LORD, with the exception of chapter 13 verse 7, which looks back to Calvary's Cross and Christ's suffering there, and they all centre in the city of Jerusalem. Here are some of the most significant prophecies concerning the future in the whole of the Old Testament revelation. Chapter 12 may be divided into two sections: first, verses 1-9 predict the future siege of Jerusalem and the LORD's deliverance of Israel then; secondly, verses 10-14 predict the national repentance and mourning of Israel when they see Christ coming again.

1. Israel's Deliverance in the Future Siege of Jerusalem, verses 1-9.

In verse 1, it is undoubtedly significant that Zechariah refers to the almighty creatorial power of the LORD who gave him this prophetic message, because it assures us that He is well able to fulfil all the predictions contained in its three chapters. Many sincere believers have doubted that they will be literally fulfilled, let alone unbelieving readers of them. We need to learn the lesson that, 'nothing is impossible with God'. The omnipotent and omniscient God who stretched forth the heavens and laid the foundation of the earth, then formed the spirit of man within him, can easily deliver Israel from their deadly enemies and bring them to the point of conversion after centuries of unbelief.

The Middle East problem, namely, the ownership of the Promised Land, and of Jerusalem in particular, has for many years been an intractable diplomatic impasse, with competing claims from both the Arabs and the Jews. In the end times it will lead to the campaign of Armageddon and the siege of Jerusalem, as is described here. From here onwards in the prophecy the phrase 'in that day', or 'the Day of the LORD, occurs eighteen times. This is the time when the LORD in the Person of His Son, the Lord Jesus Christ, will intervene in this world's affairs and judge mankind prior to His Millennial Kingdom. According to verses 2-3, the LORD will make His city of Jerusalem a 'cup of trembling' to all the nations who gather around it to capture it, that is, it will become the means of His pouring out His wrath on them, and making them stagger like a drunken man. Further, the LORD will make Jerusalem a 'burdensome stone' to all nations who come to fight against it, too heavy for them to lift and deal with. All who then attempt to lift it will be severely injured; the problem of Jerusalem and Israel will be too great for them to cope with or solve by any means, including military might. As Isaiah said years before, 'no weapon that is formed against thee (Israel) shall prosper'; see Isaiah 54. 17. Then the LORD will fight for His earthly people as never before, when they are surrounded by the armies of all the other nations on earth.

Verse 4 predicts the LORD's action in the battles that follow the siege of Jerusalem. The weaponry described is that of ancient battles, not modern warfare. We do not know whether, or not, in the time of the Great Tribulation, contemporary modern weaponry will still be available, or whether the prophet is using the language of his own day to describe a war which might be fought with more sophisticated weapons than those mentioned here. At all events, there will be a supernatural element in the LORD's intervention in the coming siege. Every horse will be struck with terror, and his rider with madness. Further, the LORD will act to help His people Judah in the battle by smiting every horse with blindness.

The result of this act of God will be that the leaders of the army of Judah will be encouraged to fight on. They will realise that they have a strong support in the form of the inhabitants of Jerusalem, since they are evidently being helped by the Almighty LORD of hosts Himself. They will realise in faith that there is divine empowerment available for victory over their countless enemies. Accordingly, in verses 6-8, the LORD will enable these leaders of His people Judah's army to overcome their enemies like a firepan in a woodpile, and like a blazing torch among sheaves of corn.

They will devour all the peoples surrounding Jerusalem with the greatest ease, and Jerusalem will be inhabited by the LORD's people as it used to be. The LORD will save the people of Judah first, that is, the people outside the city walls of Jerusalem. This is to ensure that the influential house of David, the royal household, and the proud city dwellers do not exalt themselves above the humbler country folk. Then the LORD will intervene in the defence of the city dwellers also in their turn, so that even the weakest among them will be empowered to fight like David and like God Himself in the form of the Angel of the LORD, the pre-incarnate Christ. They will be granted superhuman strength. Verse 9 then summarises this section by saying that the LORD's aim will be to destroy all the nations who have come against Jerusalem. Israel's deliverance will be total and due to the LORD alone.

2. Israel's National Repentance, Conversion, and Mourning at Christ's Second Coming, verses 10-14.

As a result of the international attack of the Gentile nations upon Jerusalem and Israel, and because Israel will suddenly realise that the LORD is fighting for them in the Person of their divine Messiah, the returning Lord Jesus Christ, the purged remnant of the nation will be saved through a vision of the crucified Christ, and undergo a thorough and sudden national conversion that will lead to their being cleansed morally and spiritually of sin and idolatry. This section of the prophecy continues into chapter 13 as far as verse 6, but here we shall confine our comments to verses 10-14.

In verse 10, the LORD, the Messiah Himself, foretells the moment when He will pour upon both the leaders and the common people of Israel the Spirit of grace and supplication which will lead them to repentance as they recognise the One who has delivered them to be the crucified Lord Jesus Christ. This is the moment in Israel's sad and chequered history when they will realise their tragic mistake and crime committed against their Saviour at His first coming in grace and humility, and they will change their attitude towards Him decisively and completely. Israel will at last look on Him Whom they pierced so cruelly and unjustly, and mourn for Him with a mourning that can only lead to thorough repentance and confession of their sin. Zechariah is here alluding to Joel's prophecy of the outpouring of the Holy Spirit in the Day of the LORD; see Joel 2. 28-29. This Scripture emphasises the fact that, unless a person is worked upon by the Holy Spirit Himself, he or she will never change their attitude towards Christ and His Father, repent, and be converted. Conviction of sin by the Holy Spirit always precedes genuine conversion, and this is the result of divine and sovereign grace alone. The apostle John applies verse 10 to the pierced and smitten Christ; see John 19. 37. These verses contrast Israel's treatment of their Messiah at His first coming, when He was rejected and killed, with their treatment of Him at His second coming, when He will be welcomed and exalted.

This day of Christ's appearing to the Jewish nation will be the fulfilment of Israel's Day of Atonement in Leviticus chapters 16 and 23, when the whole nation fasted and mourned all day for their sins. Verses 10-14 predict Israel's mourning in repentance in great detail. It will be universal and intense. Verse 10 describes it as like that for an only firstborn son, the lost heir of the family and its prime hope for the future. In verse 11, it is likened to that for King Josiah, the last good king and hope of the Judaean dynasty, who was killed, apparently at Hadadrimmon in the plain of Megiddo, by Pharaoh Neco II of Egypt, when he unwisely intervened in an international dispute between Egypt and Assyria; 2 Kings 23. 29-30. Every family will mourn deeply throughout the whole land, from the house of David, the royal family, to the house of Nathan, either the son of David or the prophet of that name, and the house of Levi and Shimei, the priestly family. Individuals within each family will mourn apart from one another; everyone will want to put themselves right with God and Christ personally and individually. There will be utter sincerity in their repentance, never to be repented of again. Therefore, from now on the LORD will be able to bless His people Israel as never before. Sorrow for sin always leads to intense joy and delight in Christ. Those who have been forgiven much, usually love their Saviour most in responsive gratitude.

CHAPTER 13

The Prophecy of Israel's National Cleansing from their Moral Sin and Idolatry, Followed by the Smiting of the LORD's True Shepherd, the Consequent Scattering and Judgement of His Sheep, and the Final Refining of Israel in the Fires of the Great Tribulation

Chapter 13 may be best divided into two main sections: first, verses 1-6 predict the national cleansing of Israel at the beginning of the Millennial Kingdom; secondly, verses 7-9 predict the death of the Good Shepherd, Christ, under the LORD's judgement, the devastating effect of this on His sheep, and, finally, how the LORD will purge His people Israel in the sufferings of the coming Great Tribulation. Each main division can profitably be further subdivided into two or three smaller units. The chapter as a whole prepares the way for the appearing of Christ in glory to reign in the Millennial Kingdom in chapter 14.

1. The LORD's Prediction of Israel's Cleansing from their Moral Sin and Uncleanness, verse 1.

In the Day of the LORD, at the beginning of Christ's intervention in this world in judgement and blessing, a fountain of water will be opened for Israel's moral cleansing from all their sins. This fountain is a symbolical way of describing the role of Christ as Israel's Saviour-Redeemer at that time. From that moment of Christ's second coming it will be open to all who desire to be cleansed from their natural uncleanness in God's sight. It will be effective for all who trust in His work of salvation on the Cross of Calvary at His first coming. Both the royal house of David and the ordinary citizens of Jerusalem will avail themselves of the LORD's provision for their salvation and cleansing, and become at once a complete nation of saved people. Believers in Christ today during the Church Age have long enjoyed this salvation through faith many years before the LORD's earthly people Israel will do so as a whole.

2. The LORD's Eradication of Idolatry and False Prophets from the Land at the Beginning of the Millennial Kingdom, verses 2-6.

Then also the land of Israel will be purged from all idolatry. During the Tribulation idolatry will again be introduced into Israel, especially in the form of the image of the Beast in the rebuilt temple in Jerusalem, the so-called Abomination of Desolation, which all men will be commanded to worship on pain of death; Revelation 13.15. At the beginning of the Millennial Kingdom of Christ, however, all idols and unclean demonic spirits will be banished from the earth. We know from Revelation chapter 20 verses 1-3 that Satan himself will be confined to the bottomless pit during the entire Millennium, and thus be rendered powerless to tempt men to sin further. Verse 2 of this chapter confirms that his emissaries will also be rendered powerless to continue their deadly work then. Also, verse 3 says that, if anyone claims to be a prophet falsely during Christ's kingdom, he will be summarily executed by his parents themselves for deception. They will thrust him through. The word used here is the same as is used in chapter 12 verse 10 of the crucifixion of Christ. So seriously will all idolatry and false prophecy be regarded then. The result will be that all false prophets will be ashamed of their pretended visions, nor will they attempt to deceive men by wearing a hairy garment, like a wolf in sheep's clothing. The prevailing atmosphere of truth and righteousness in the Millennial Kingdom will cause all who are false prophets to deny that they ever were prophets at all, but claim that they had always been ordinary working men, like farmers. When they are challenged about the self-inflicted wounds in their body, which are really the evidence of idolatrous practices, they will claim that they were disciplined by their friends or family members. Although some commentators see in verse 6 a reference to the wounds of Christ, the preceding context of the false prophets suggests that the theme of the false prophets is being continued here. It is probably not a reference to the True Prophet-Messiah, Christ, despite the clear reference to Him in the next verse.

3. The LORD's Prediction of the Smiting of His Own Son, the Good Shepherd of Israel, at Calvary's Cross and its Devastating Effect on His Sheep, verse 7.

This verse does clearly refer to Christ, the True Good Shepherd of Israel, the LORD's chosen Leader of His people. It tells us that the basis of Israel's cleansing was the smiting of Christ by God His Father on the Cross of Calvary for our sins. Christ had always been the LORD's close Fellow, or Companion, in eternity, but the LORD judged Him for our sins, in order that we might be saved and cleansed from them by faith in Him. The Triune Deity cooperated in accomplishing our salvation out of pure love for us, though we are all unworthy. Amazing grace of God! The result of Christ, the Shepherd of Israel, being smitten on Calvary was that His sheep, the people of Israel, were scattered in a worldwide dispersion, as we still find today. Also, the end of verse 7 warns us that the LORD turned His hand against (not 'upon' AV) the little ones of the flock, that is, the believing remnant among the Jews. Just as their True Shepherd had been persecuted and killed by His enemies, so the LORD would allow those of them who believed on the Saviour when He came the first time to be subjected to suffering and martyrdom by their contemporaries. Initially, this may refer to the sufferings of the early Christian Jews in the Book of the Acts. However, it probably primarily refers to the sufferings of the Jews during their worldwide dispersion.

4. The Prediction of Israel's Final Refining from Defilement in the Sufferings of the Great Tribulation, verses 8-9.

Just as in chapter 11, where the prophet Zechariah moves from the rejection of Christ by the nation of Israel to the judgement of God for this unbelief in the Great Tribulation, so here we have the smiting of the Shepherd followed by the time of Jacob's trouble. A great gap exists between verse 7 and verses 8-9, the whole of the Church Age in fact. These verses cannot refer to the sufferings of the Jews during the siege of Jerusalem in AD 70, but look on to the Great Tribulation, when the Antichrist, or Beast, will persecute them unmercifully and many of them will die. Two-thirds of the nation will die, but a third will survive and form the nucleus of the believing remnant who enter the Millennial Kingdom in their mortal bodies. This surviving remnant will be refined by the fires of persecution as in a fiery furnace like silver and gold, and will be purified by the process. It will create faith in them and lead them to call upon the name of the LORD in their distress for salvation, and the LORD will hear and answer their prayers for help. The LORD will again acknowledge Israel to be His people, while they will acknowledge Him to be their LORD God again. The relationship between them and the LORD will be completely restored, and the remnant will be delivered in their hour of deep distress.

CHAPTER 14

The Final Deliverance of Jerusalem from Extinction in the Siege of All Nations at Armageddon by the Intervention of Christ when He Comes Again to the Mount of Olives, Followed by its Geographical and Judgemental Effects, and Conditions of Worship and Holiness during the Millennial Kingdom of Christ over the Whole World

This closing chapter of Zechariah's prophecy has been rightly called 'The Grand Finale'. It concludes his second major oracle, or prophetic message, which has almost entirely concerned the second coming of Christ. It begins with a scene of total and universal war, and finishes with a scene of total and universal peace. Its reference is wholly future to us today, and it should be understood as literally as human language will allow us to do so. In it Christ takes absolute control of the critical situation which He finds when He returns, and begins to reign over the whole world in complete righteousness, holiness, truth, and peace. If words mean anything, there is going to be a literal kingdom of Christ on earth after His glorious second coming. This chapter predicts the triumphant return of Israel's once-rejected Messiah as the divine KING OF KINGS AND LORD OF LORDS.

Chapter 14 may be divided into several sections for convenience of comment. Verses 1-3 predict the coming of the LORD in the Person of Christ to deliver Jerusalem from imminent defeat by the surrounding nations of the whole world at the height of the campaign of Armageddon. Verses 4-7 predict the return of Christ to the Mount of Olives and its accompanying geographical effects and climatic conditions. Verses 8-11 further predict geographical changes around Jerusalem at the time when the LORD becomes King over the whole earth. Verses 12-15 describe the previous destruction of Israel's enemies in further detail. Verses 16-19 describe worship during the Millennial Kingdom by all nations. Finally, verses 20-21 describe the holiness of Judah and Jerusalem during Christ's reign on earth.

1. The LORD's Deliverance of Jerusalem from Imminent Defeat, verses 1-3.

Verse 1 declares that there is coming a day that is peculiarly and pre-eminently the LORD's. The reference here to the Day of the LORD is unique in its phrasing. We should note that throughout the whole chapter the Person who is clearly the Lord Jesus Christ, since His feet are said to stand on the Mount of Olives in verse 4, is referred to as the LORD, Jehovah, Israel's covenant-keeping God Himself. So Christ and the Messiah who delivers Israel is the same as God. This strengthens the abundant evidence in Scripture for the Deity of Christ. On this Day of the LORD, here the height of the Great Tribulation, Israel is being plundered by the besieging armies of the nations attacking her, and is on the point of total defeat. They are dividing the plunder of Jerusalem amongst themselves just before the LORD intervenes.

Verse 2 explains that it is the LORD who has brought all the Gentile nations to fight Jerusalem, not just Satan and his demonic agents. This is the campaign of Armageddon spoken about in the book of Revelation chapters 14 and 16. Satan and wicked men may have their own plans against God's people, but it is the LORD who is controlling them for His own purposes. This is His final showdown with rebellious mankind and Satan's forces before the Millennium. Jerusalem will have been captured by their enemies, the homes plundered, the womenfolk abused, and half the population will be in the process of being deported into exile, but there will be a remnant in the city still who have not yet been killed. It may be this remnant that is referred to in chapter 12 as fighting like heroes with the LORD's help; for chapter 12 probably describes part of the same scene.

Verse 3 then says that this is the moment when the LORD, that is, the Messiah, Christ, intervenes and fights for His people. He is coming as the Divine Warrior (foretold in the prophetical Scriptures) to destroy all His enemies once and for all. According to other Scriptures, such as Matthew chapter 24, Christ will be seen descending in the clouds down to earth to save His people in their desperate hour of need. This also is the moment when His people will look on Him as the One whom they pierced and mourn in repentance for Him.

2. *The Return of Christ to the Mount of Olives and its Effects, verses 4-7.*

Verse 4 predicts that Christ's feet, once nail-pierced in rejection, will touch down on the Mount of Olives, the very same place from which He ascended to heaven after His glorious resurrection; see Acts 1. 11. This time He has come to judge and reign forever over His creation. When His feet touch the mountain, it will cleave into two halves in the direction east to west, leaving a great valley permanently available for the surviving Israelites to escape through to safety from the attacking armies. This upheaval will be caused by a great earthquake, such as occurred apparently in the days of King Uzziah in the eighth century BC. Geologists have confirmed that there is already a distinct fault-line in the Mount of Olives running east-west, as is described here, which could easily open up under the pressure of an earthquake. The scene has already been set for this cataclysmic event. The location of Azal (or Azel RV) is not known. The valley may be the same as the so-called Valley of Jehoshaphat mentioned in Joel chapter 3 verse 2 in this connection as the place where Christ will judge the nations after His second coming.

Verse 5 further says that this will be when the LORD, Zechariah's God, will come, and that all the saints will be with Him. We know from other Scriptures that the Church saints will accompany Christ at His second coming, although they will not participate in the campaign of Armageddon; see 1 Thessalonians 3. 13; Jude 14; Revelation 19. 11-16. We surely anticipate with joy that day of Christ's vindication and Israel's deliverance.

Verses 6-7 indicate that the day of the LORD's coming will be unique in its climatic conditions, being neither light nor dark, but unclear all day. By the evening of that momentous day, however, it will be light again. Again, we know from other Scriptures that there will be disturbances in the heavenly bodies, including the sun and the moon, just before Christ returns in glory; see Isaiah 13. 10; 34. 4; Joel 2. 10, 30-31; 3. 15; Matthew 24. 29.

3. Other Geographical Changes at the Time when Christ becomes Universal King, verses 8-11.

First of all, verse 8 predicts that there will be living rivers of water flowing out from Jerusalem, from the threshold of the new Millennial Temple in fact, which will divide and go partly east into the Dead Sea, and partly west into the Mediterranean Sea. It will be a supernatural river, since it becomes deeper as it progresses without having any tributaries, and will refresh the waters of the Dead Sea, so that fishing will be possible there once again. Jerusalem will be its watershed. The other Scriptures which predict this river are Ezekiel 47. 1-12, Joel 3. 18, and Psalm 46. 4. While this river is a literal one, it also symbolises the spiritual blessings which will flow out from Christ during His Millennial reign to the whole earth.

Verse 9 asserts that in that day the LORD, in the Person of Christ His incarnate Son, will be king over the whole world, and He will be the only One worshipped throughout the world, for the first time in history. There will be no more idolatry.

Verses 10-11 inform us that the whole land of Judah will be supernaturally levelled to become a plain, and the damage done by various earth-movements and wars during the Tribulation will be restored, so that people will be able to live there and in Jerusalem in perfect security. Jerusalem will be elevated above its present level, and thus become more prominent from a distance, as will befit the future capital city of the world, Christ's capital; see Isaiah 2. 2-3; Micah 4. 1-2.

4. The Previous Destruction of Israel's Enemies, verses 12-15.

Verses 12-15 look back to verse 2, the time of the siege of Jerusalem, when the LORD comes out to fight Israel's enemies. The LORD will use three weapons to destroy His enemies. First, He will send a deadly plague upon them, similar to a horrible leprosy. Secondly, He will send a great panic into their hearts, which will cause them to fight one another, rather than the Israelites. Thirdly, He will empower the Jews with superhuman power and courage to fight back at their attackers and to capture an immense quantity of plunder for themselves in the form of silver, gold, and garments. Much of this may be booty which the enemies have just taken from their fellow-Jews in their initial attack. Verse 15 says that the plague will affect all the attackers' animals as well as the men and women among them.

5. Universal Worship of the LORD during the Millennium, verses 16-19.

The terrible judgements which will precede the establishment of Christ's kingdom will presumably have taught righteousness to the survivors of both Israel and the Gentile nations by turning them in faith and obedience to Christ as their Saviour and universal King. Certainly, other Scriptures teach that no-one who is not born again will enter the Millennial Kingdom alive; see John 3. 3; Matthew 25. 31-46. Verse 16 here predicts that all these believing and repentant survivors will come up to Jerusalem annually to worship the LORD there, and to keep the Feast of Tabernacles, the Jewish feast which foreshadowed the joy of harvest, rest, and thanksgiving. We know from Ezekiel chapter 45 that the Feast of Tabernacles will continue to be celebrated during the Millennial Kingdom, which it typified, among a few others of the Jewish feasts which will not have been superseded by that time. Christ is here called both the LORD of hosts and the King.

Verses 17-19 give a warning that, if any of the surviving nations refuse to come up to observe the Feast of Tabernacles in Jerusalem, they will be punished providentially by the LORD withholding rain from them. If the Egyptians, or any of the other nations, fail to obey this command of the LORD, not only will the LORD withhold rain from them, but He will also strike them with a plague. Egypt has until now been largely dependent for water on the flooding of the River Nile, rather than on direct rainfall, but the Egyptians would certainly be affected seriously by the plague. Perhaps improved climatic conditions in the Millennium will also somewhat change the situation in Egypt then. Rebellious sin will be punished very severely and promptly during the Millennial Kingdom. It will no longer be the present Day of God's Grace.

6. The Holiness of the Millennial Kingdom, verses 20-21.

The last two verses of the prophecy stand in stark contrast with its call to repentance in chapter 1. There the LORD's people were exhorted to forsake their sins and live differently. Here we see a predicted world scene which is characterised throughout by conformity with the LORD's own holiness. Because the believers who survive into the Millennial Kingdom in their mortal bodies will still have innately sinful natures, there will still be sin and outbreaks of rebellion in that day, which will be judged summarily. Memorial sacrifices will need to be offered for breaches of the LORD's moral laws, although they will only be effective in reconciling those who commit sinful actions by the retrospective virtue of Christ's one sacrifice for sins forever on Calvary's Cross; see Ezekiel chapters 40-45. The predominant characteristic of the Millennium will be holy living which accords with the holiness of Christ the King. Holiness will characterise both public life: the bells of the horses; religious life: the cooking pots in the LORD's house; and private life: every domestic pot in Jerusalem and Judah. The latter will even be fit to be used for cooking sacrifices in the Millennial Temple; so clean will they be. Finally, there will no longer be any people unfit to worship the LORD in the temple, such as the morally degenerate, dishonest, and unclean Canaanites. Everything and everyone will be in conformity with the holy character of the LORD of hosts who will have saved, cleansed, and restored them to their rightful position as a priestly nation for the LORD's glory, worship and service. Because He is the Holy One of Israel, the LORD will establish holiness throughout His millennial world! Hallelujah! Amen!

Conclusion

As the Wise Man said: 'Let us hear the conclusion of the whole matter'
(Ecclesiastes 12.13).

This, then, will be the result, 'When the LORD Remembers His Own'. Upon His people Israel's sincere repentance, He will be both able and willing to save them from all their sins and the consequences of them, to cleanse them by the blood of Christ's sacrifice, and to fit them again to worship and to serve Him in a priestly capacity as a redeemed and sanctified nation. Zechariah's Prophecy clearly predicts that this will happen to the LORD's earthly people Israel, when He resumes His relationship with them, after the present Church Age has ended in the Rapture. Israel certainly has a future and a sure hope of having the glory of the LORD in their midst once again. Their believing remnant will be saved on the same basis as we are, that is, by faith in Christ's vicarious sacrifice on Calvary's Cross, and, during Christ's Millennial Kingdom, will act as the LORD's servants to proclaim His Name and worth to all nations on earth then. So they still have an ultimately glorious future role to play in the LORD's purposes of grace and judgement, and no-one will be able to frustrate the LORD from fulfilling it for Him.

However, as members of the LORD's parallel heavenly people, the New Testament Church of the Age of Grace, Christian believers today are meant to learn many valuable spiritual lessons from these divine predictions concerning Israel's restoration. The LORD God of Israel is still the God of recovery and the second opportunity to respond to His calls for repentance, if we, like Israel, have strayed away from Him. The LORD will remember us also, the New Testament 'His Own', and will act to accomplish our full spiritual restoration. As He said to Israel through the prophet Joel, 'I will restore to you the years that the locust hath eaten' (Joel 2. 25), and reintegrate us into His service. The key to restoration, however, is our sincere repentance from all our sinful ways which have brought us into bondage to sin and loss of fellowship with our Lord. Therefore, if we should find that this situation is ours, we need to heed the exhortation of the Lord Jesus to the local church at Ephesus, that is, 'Remember therefore from whence thou art fallen, and repent, and do the first works', out of 'first love' for Him; see Revelation 2. 4-5. If we do this, then the LORD can and will bring us back, like Israel, into blessing untold, and a future life of useful service for His glory, until Christ comes again for all of us. Yes, God is the God of the seeming impossible! Praise His Name!

When the LORD remembers His Own

When the LORD remembers His Own